On Consulting the Faithful
in Matters of Doctrine

On Consulting the Faithful in Matters of Doctrine

JOHN HENRY NEWMAN

EDITED WITH AN INTRODUCTION BY
JOHN COULSON

A SHEED & WARD BOOK

ROWMAN & LITTLEFIELD PUBLISHERS, INC.
Lanham • Boulder • New York • Toronto • Oxford

Nihil Obstat: Carolus Davis, S.T.L.
          Censor deputatus
Imprimatur: E. Morrogh Bernard, Vic. Gen.
Westmonasterii, die 31a Octobris, 1961

> The Nihil Obstat and Imprimatur are a declaration that a book or pamphlet is considered to be free from doctrinal or moral error. It is not implied that those who have granted the Nihil Obstat and Imprimatur agree with the contents, opinions or statements expressed.

A SHEED & WARD BOOK

ROWMAN & LITTLEFIELD PUBLISHERS, INC.

Published in the United States of America
by Rowman & Littlefield Publishers, Inc.
A wholly owned subsidary of The Rowman & Littlefield Publishing Group, Inc.
4501 Forbes Boulevard, Suite 200, Lanham, Maryland 20706
www.rowmanlittlefield.com

PO Box 317
Oxford
OX2 9RU, UK

British Library Cataloguing in Publication Information Available

The Sheed & Ward edition of this book was cataloged as follows by the Library of Congress:

Library of Congress Catalog Card Number 62-9877
ISBN- 13: 978-0-934134-51-4
ISBN- 10: 0-934134-51-0

Printed in the United States of America

CONTENTS

EDITOR'S NOTE

This introduction forms part of a larger work, *The Church and the Laity,* to be published shortly.

It is based to a considerable extent on hitherto unpublished material, so that in order to keep footnotes to the minimum, references are cited only when they give a different account from that available in Ward's *Life of Newman,* or refer directly to unpublished material.

References

Butler.   Dom Cuthbert Butler: *Life of Bishop Ulla-thorne* (Burns and Oates: 1926).

Bishop.   Marginal manuscript annotations to Gasquet's *Lord Acton and his circle* made by Edmund Bishop (Downside Abbey Archives).

G.   A. Gasquet: *Lord Acton and his circle* (Burns and Oates: 1906).

Simpson.   A letter written by Simpson for Montalambert's *Le Correspondant,* but probably never published. On internal evidence it would seem to have been written in April 1859. (Downside Abbey Archives).

W.   Dom Aelred Watkin and Professor Herbert Butterfield: "Gasquet and the Acton-Simpson Correspondence" *Cambridge Historical Journal,* vol. x, no. 1, 1950.

O.   Archives of the Birmingham Oratory.

Acknowledgements

I am particularly grateful to the Abbot of Downside for his advice, and for so kindly permitting me to use the library and reproduce material in the archives; and to the Very Reverend Father Stephen Dessain, Superior of the Birmingham Oratory, for his most helpful criticisms, and for so generously making available all the relevant material, especially that on Newman and Gillow, and for allowing its publication.

I wish also to thank Father Damian McElrath, Mr Lancelot Sheppard, Dom Hilary Steuart, Mr David Stokes, Dom Illtyd Trethowan, and Dom Aelred Watkin for their most valuable advice and assistance.

John Coulson

INTRODUCTION

INTRODUCTION

On Consulting the Faithful in Matters of Doctrine was published by Newman in the *Rambler* for July 1859; and part of it, with some additions and amendments, was re-printed in 1871 as an appendix to the third edition of *The Arians of the Fourth Century.* Although it has recently (1940) been translated into German, it has never been re-published in England; and the present edition is the first in any language to contain a collated version of both the 1859 and 1871 texts.

This work is fundamental not only to a fuller understanding of Newman's theory of doctrinal development, but to an appreciation of the importance he attaches to the laity in his theology. It also provides the reasons for his silence as a Catholic writer between the publication of the *Lectures and Essays on University Subjects* in 1858 and the writing of the *Apologia* in 1864, as well as helping to explain why Kingsley's attack produced such a volcanic reply. Yet although the re-publication of so important a work has been long over-due, the delay may have been inevitable. Today, lay initiative is everywhere on the increase; it has received unprecedented papal encouragement; and it has had for its formation such works as Père Congar's *Lay People in the Church.* In Newman's day, however, the reverse was true;

and his publication of this essay was an act of political suicide from which his career within the Church was never fully to recover; at one stroke he, whose reputation as the one honest broker between the extremes of English Catholic opinion had hitherto stood untarnished, gained the Pope's personal displeasure, the reputation at Rome of being the most dangerous man in England, and a formal accusation of heresy preferred against him by the Bishop of Newport.

When, in November 1858, Newman retired from the rectorship of the Catholic University, he hoped that he would be left alone to write a sustained and substantial work of theology; but he was to be drawn almost immediately, and once more against his will, into a controversy which was to involve all those principles for which he had fought so fruitlessly in Ireland.

A Catholic periodical, the *Rambler,* which had been started by an Oxford convert, J. M. Capes, in 1848 was now being edited jointly by another Oxford convert clergyman, Richard Simpson, and by the young Sir John Acton, who had joined Simpson as co-editor at the age of twenty-three in 1857. Although the circulation of such a paper was small (the number for May 1859 sold just over 800 copies, and the editors considered 1,000 to be a very healthy figure), its influence was out of all proportion to its circulation. Its aim was to re-habilitate Catholic thought in a non-Catholic world, and it did so by combining standards of scholarship previously unknown in Catholic journalism with attitudes critical of ecclesiastical authority which had become equally uncustomary. By the beginning of 1859 it became certain that, unless special measures were taken, the Review would be censured in the forthcoming Pastorals of the English Bishops. Both sides turned to Newman as the only acceptable intermediary.

One of the alleged sources of irritation had been the style in which many of the articles in the *Rambler* had been written; and for this Richard Simpson was held to be responsible: "he writes about the Church in a sort of sore tone, and at times as if from without," wrote a Catholic layman to Newman; and Newman's first task was to persuade Simpson to resign, on condition that the threat of censure would be withdrawn. Since the co-editor, Acton, was equally unacceptable to the authorities, Newman was left with the reward traditionally reserved to over-scrupulous intermediaries: either he must bring the *Rambler* to an end, or himself become its editor.

So runs the accepted version of the dispute; but a closer examination and fresh evidence seem to indicate a more complex background.

In the *Rambler* for June 1858 had appeared a strong letter from Canon Tierney criticising the reviewer of Wiseman's *Recollections of the last four Popes* for accepting Wiseman's denial that the historian Lingard had been made a Cardinal by Leo XII. This criticism proved to be mistaken, but although an apology was made, the Cardinal remained offended and suspicious. The August number contained a brief review by Acton of Chéruel's *Marie Stuart and Catherine de Medici*, in which Acton asserted that "no Catholic is as good as his religion". He illustrated his contention, somewhat casually, with the remark, "nor because St Augustine was the greatest doctor of the West, need we conceal the fact that he was also the father of Jansenism". This raised such a storm that when, in September, Döllinger came to stay with Acton, he was persuaded to provide the evidence and a theological justification for the remark, which was published as a letter in the *Rambler* for December.

In the light of the subsequent retractions and modifications, Acton's own position is worth noting. Writing to Simpson in September 1858, he says:

"Döllinger, who is here, is fattening with laughter at the ignorance of our divines betrayed in the Augustinian dispute. . . . . I do most deliberately hold that errors condemned by the Church are to be found in the works of the Doctor Gratiae."[1]

Acton furthermore wrote to Wiseman in November, saying (according to a letter to Simpson) that "he must prepare for a stunning reply next no. which would astonish rather than offend and which tho' it would not convert enemies, would most certainly satisfy your Eminence whose blessing etc, etc"[2]. But the Cardinal was not satisfied, and Döllinger's letter was delated to Rome. Acton went to see Newman to tell him the news of this, and they had a long talk together in the December. The relevant parts of Acton's letter to Simpson, describing this meeting and Newman's attitude, have never previously been reproduced in an unexpurgated form:

"I had a 3 hours talk with the venerable Noggs, who came out at last with his real sentiments to an extent which startled me with respect both to things and persons, as

[1] W. p. 88[11]
[2] W. p. 89

H. E. (Wiseman), Ward, Dalgairns, etc, etc; natural inclination of men in power to tyrannize; ignorance and presumption of our would-be theologians, in short what you and I would say comfortably over a glass of whiskey. I did not think he would ever cast aside his diplomacy and buttonment so entirely, and was quite surprised at the intense interest he betrayed in the Rambler. He was quite miserable when I told him the news and moaned for a long time, rocking himself backwards and forwards over the fire, like an old woman with a toothache . . . He thinks the move provoked both by the hope of breaking down the R(ambler) and by jealousy of Döllinger. He asked whether we suspected the Jesuits or Errington, and at last inclined to the notion that the source is in Brompton. He has no present advice, being ignorant of the course of such affairs in Rome, and not believing much security to be in the right in such cases, except that we should declare, if you can make up your mind to do so, that we do not treat theology in our pages. . . . He is most friendly, and considered the Rambler invaluable, to be kept 'in terrorem', according to Madame Swetchine's answer to the 'vers Latin, Quis custodiet custodes?' for the authorities."[1]

Although it was Acton who wrote the offending sentence about St Augustine, it was Simpson who was made the scapegoat for all the Rambler's delinquencies. Edmund Bishop's comment on the affair is contained in a pencilled note at the foot of a letter written from Acton to Simpson in February 1859:

"And so Acton within a few days 'disappeared' from England, leaving Simpson, alone, to meet the storm which

[1] Downside Abbey Archives

Acton, contrary to S's views, had raised. —S., poor wretch, was only a convert.—By the end of February, Simpson had been already *smashed.*"[1]

It was not until 21 March 1859, that Newman made his decision to edit the *Rambler*. It had taken weeks of prayer and deliberation, and he may have been moved to it by the fear of what Simpson would do if the *Rambler* ceased to be carried on, since Simpson had threatened that if his resignation destroyed the review, he would make the whole affair public and claim compensation from the Bishops for financial loss. Newman accepted the *Rambler* as "a bitter penance", and only at the express wish of Bishop Ullathorne and Cardinal Wiseman. His short term policy was to take it out of the front line of controversy.

"Let it go back to its own literary line," he had written to Acton in December 1858. "Let it be instructive, clever and amusing. Let it cultivate a general temper of good humour and courtesy. Let it praise as many persons as it can, and gain friends in neutral quarters, and become the organ of others by the interest it has made them take in its proceeding. Then it will be able to plant a good blow at a fitting time with great effect."

Newman believed that the review had placed itself in its present false position for three reasons: it had treated of theology proper, it had done so in magazine fashion, and it had allowed laymen to do so. "It requires an explanation when a layman writes on theology", and given the existing difficulties of the Holy See, especially in a missionary country such as England, a layman could only write in its support; to publish criticisms of authority was to court

[1] Bishop p. 59

inevitable disaster, and for a convert, like Simpson, to do so was merely to substantiate the general proposition: "all converts are dangerous".

Newman still believed that, without compromising principle, a different tone and choice of subjects were possible,—(to read the *Rambler* today is to wonder what all the fuss was about)—, but Acton's ironical comment that "people are quite as sensitive about other things as about theology"[1] was closer to the truth.

In his Advertisement to the new series of the *Rambler*, Newman was at pains to do nothing which would "damage the fair fame of men who I believed were at bottom sincere Catholics". Newman thought it "unfair, ungenerous, impertinent, and cowardly to make in their behalf acts of confession and contrition"; and he deliberately avoided saying anything about changes in matter, drift, objects, and tone.

The first of the new series, for May 1859, seems innocuous enough. It begins with a review article, entitled *The Mission of the Isles of the North,* on the sermons, lectures, and speeches, delivered by the Cardinal Archbishop in the course of his late tour in Ireland. The treacle of eulogy is spread thick indeed. "No other public man in England," we are told, "could have answered to the demand thus made upon his stores of mind with the spirit and the intellectual power which the Cardinal (Wiseman) displayed on the occasion." There are other articles on the *Religious Associations in the Sixteenth Century,* the *Development of Gothic Architecture,* the *Ancient Saints,* and one by the Baron d'Eckstein on Lammenais. There are certain Literary Notices, in one of which appears *Lectures and Essays on*

[1] G. pp. 49, 51

2

University Subjects by John Henry Newman, to which the feeling comment is appended that "it does but supply another instance of (the author's) lot all through life, to have been led to its publication not on any matured plan or by any view of his own, but by the duties or the circumstances of the moment".

But this appeal was passed over by those close but unsympathetic readers who were concerned only to find grounds for their prejudice that the new series would be no different from the old. There were only two points in that May issue which could have been selected for attack : a letter in the correspondence section which ended with the question : "how far is it allowable, or desirable, for laymen to study theology?"; and certain remarks buried deep in the small type and double columns of the commentary on Contemporary Events. Unsigned, they were written by Newman as editor, and dealt with the judgement of the English Bishops on the proposed Royal Commission on elementary education. They contained the following remarks :

"we do unfeignedly believe . . . that their Lordships really desire to know the opinion of the laity on subjects in which the laity are especially concerned. *If even in the preparation of a dogmatic definition the faithful are consulted,* as lately in the instance of the Immaculate Conception, it is at least as natural to anticipate such an act of kind feeling and sympathy in great practical questions." (my italics)

This passage, and in particular that part of it in italics, was the point chosen by the *Rambler's* opponents, of whom the chief was that professor of theology at Ushaw, Dr Gillow, who had previously reported Döllinger's article to the authorities. It was a sound tactical choice, as the Bishops were extremely sensitive to the education question, and had been exposed to some pertinent and expert criticism in previous numbers of the *Rambler*; and if we are to understand why Newman felt it necessary to defend contributions to the old series of the *Rambler* in the first number of the new, it is necessary to know something about a question, which, even now, is not without its contemporary significance.

The state of public elementary education was causing such concern that all parties agreed that more information on the way in which existing arrangements worked was required; and in 1858 the Newcastle Commission was appointed to report on measures likely to extend "sound and cheap elementary instruction to all classes of the people". One of the main problems was how to reconcile the freedom of denominational schools with public control over the subsidies which they received.

In default of any official guidance from the Bishops, the *Rambler* had treated the matter of Catholic co-operation with the Commission as one still open to discussion, and had published two articles in January and February 1859. Although unsigned, they were written by Nasmyth Scott Stokes, the father of the inventor of the Stokes gun and grandfather of the late Richard Stokes, M.P., and himself a convert. His elder brother had been sent down from Cambridge for the double offence of getting married and joining the Roman Catholic Church; and the younger brother became a Catholic some time after coming down from Cambridge in 1844. He was called to the Bar and became the first secretary of the Catholic Poor-School Committee, a body set up to deal with the Government on behalf of the

Bishops, who were still not legally recognised. In his account, Simpson says that the real business of the committee was undertaken by Stokes, whom he describes as "a silent saturnine person", who "showed the abundance of his resources by organising out of the most heterogeneous elements the committee in question, which while seeming to obey he really guided & ruled, not by the charm of his temper nor by any unworthy arts of flattery, but by a strong will combined with a natural aptitude for affairs, a power of saying the right thing at the right moment, and a justice & accuracy of view which those least inclined to him were obliged to acknowledge. It was under the guidance of this secretary that the Committee made such advantageous terms with the government, and nothing could be more satisfactory than the progress of matters under his management."[1]

Stokes became one of the Catholic school inspectors in 1853 and was promoted senior inspector in 1871, thus making him a contemporary of Matthew Arnold in the Inspectorate. Later he served on the Royal Commission on Primary Education in Ireland. Edmund Bishop, who had known Stokes when he was working in the Education Office, says that "he was an immutably solid person to the end",[2] whilst Acton refers to him as "our prudent colleague".[3]

The *Rambler* articles certainly reflect the qualities of their author: they are expert, weighty and yet moderate in tone. They begin, it is important to note, with "due submission to ecclesiastical authority, desiring nothing but to

[1] Simpson
[2] Bishop p. lxv
[3] G. p. 240. 8 Dec. 1861

promote the welfare and progress of the Church; and we revoke and wish unsaid any word which may seem to tend in an opposite direction. ... In stating actual facts, we desire to furnish materials for a judgement rather than force a conclusion of our own."

The argument is as follows: —that although no Catholic was a member of the Commission, one could have been appointed if representations had been received in time. Failure to make such representations was the responsibility of the Catholic Poor-School Committee ("which communicates so rarely with its supporters and the public, and finds so few opportunities to rouse and inform the Catholic body upon educational questions"). Catholics should co-operate with the Commission, not only because they were in receipt of public funds and could be compelled to give evidence, if Parliament so determined, but because open co-operation would help dispel bigotry and the suspicion that "Catholics make bad citizens of a free state". A positive policy of opening wide the doors would let the world learn that building grants had been spent on schools and teachers' houses and not on churches and presbyteries, that Catholic education was not a hole and corner mixture of jugglery, immorality and sedition, but calculated beyond doubt to train useful citizens and sound Christians.

There was a deeper danger still, and this was that the existing denominational system, so complex and costly, would be superseded by some kind of state-supported schools. On these grounds Catholics should welcome the Commissioners' representatives into their schools, so that they might witness the effectiveness of their religious teaching. No principle would be conceded, because the

Commissioners were not inspectors, but appointed for a particular occasion, and they were concerned not with the matter of religious instruction but with its method. Were Catholic poor-schools so unlike others that no kind of comparison could be arrived at?

The author concludes the February article by asking what will be the consequence of Catholic isolation, if grant is withdrawn and schools of a sufficient standard cannot be provided. He cites the similar controversy taking place in the United States, and quotes from *Brownson's Review* the warning that less harm will come to a Catholic child who attends a well run state school in which he may be compelled to read the Protestant version of the Bible, than to one who is placed in a Catholic school, under half-educated and ill-paid teachers, whose manners and influence can do little to elevate or refine him, so that there will perhaps be more difficulty in preserving to the faith the children educated in such schools than those educated in the state schools of the country.

The judgement delivered by the Bishops, which Newman printed in the May *Rambler,* was supplemented by extracts from the Pastoral of Bishop Ullathorne of Birmingham, whose discussion of the subject was characteristically more thorough, cogent, and illuminating. Commissioners were no different from inspectors, a sacred and religious principle was at issue, the concession demanded was equivalent to a surrender of the very ground on which Catholic inspectors had been demanded and obtained, the distinction between matter and method was denied ("only a Catholic can understand the mind and spirit of a Catholic"), and the presence of a Commissioner's representative at religious instruction would confer upon him in the eyes of the children an impression of the state's exercising authority in matters religious. One or two, here and there, had used the public press as a weapon against the conduct of the episcopacy, and might have separated the faithful from its pastors in a matter involving ecclesiastical freedom, episcopal prudence and religious discipline.

In his editorial note, Newman immediately apologises: "we did not know that the Bishops had spoken formally." (Decisions apparently taken in the November were not communicated until the Spring). His second remark which contained the cause of all the trouble is worth quoting in full:

"Acknowledging, then, most fully the prerogatives of the episcopate, we do unfeignedly believe, both from the reasonableness of the matter, and especially from the prudence, gentleness, and considerateness which belong to them personally, that their Lordships really desire to know the opinion of the laity on subjects in which the laity are especially concerned. If even in the preparation of a dogmatic definition the faithful are consulted, as lately in the instance of the Immaculate Conception, it is at least as natural to anticipate such an act of kind feeling and sympathy in great practical questions, out of the condescension which belongs to those who are *forma facti gregis ex animo*. If our words or tone were disrespectful, we deeply grieve and apologise for such a fault; but surely we are not disrespectful in thinking, and in having thought, that the Bishops would like to know the sentiments of an influential portion of the laity before they took any step which perhaps they could not recall. Surely it was no disrespect towards them to desire that they should have the laity rallying round them on the great question of education with the imposing zeal which has lately been exemplified in Ireland, in the great meeting which was held at Cork. If we have uttered a word inconsistent with this explanation of our conduct,—if we argued in a hard or disrespectful tone,—if we put into print what might better have been conveyed to their Lordships in some other way,—we repeat, we are deeply sorry for it. We are too fully convinced of the misery of any division between the rulers of the Church and the educated laity,—we grieve too deeply, too bitterly, over such instances as are found, either in the present day or in the history of the past, of such mutual alienations,—to commit ourselves consciously to any act which may tend to so dire a clamity. It is our fervent prayer that their Lordships may live in the hearts of their people; of the poor as well as of the rich, of the rich as well as of the poor; of the clergy as well as of the laity, of the laity as well as of the clergy: but whatever be our own anxious desire on the subject, we know that the desire of the Bishops themselves is far more intense, more generous, more heart-consuming, than can be the desire of any persons, however loyal to them, who are committed to their charge. Let them pardon, then, the incidental hastiness of manner or want of ceremony of the rude Jack-tars of their vessel, as far as it occurred, in consideration of the zeal and energy with which they haul-to the ropes and man the yards."

Newman's nautical metaphor is significant. Earlier on, in speaking of his policy for the *Rambler*, he had recommended the policy of Wellington in the lines of Torres Vedras; and such naval and military metaphors come naturally to one who burned to see the Church take advantage of its emancipation and become, once again, a community on the march.

Unhappily, nothing so effectively demonstrates the dimensions of the gulf which divided not only the Bishops from the laity, but more particularly the converts from their fellow Catholics than does this clash over the education question. Converts, such as Stokes and Simpson, were more deeply committed even than they realised to those liberal assumptions which, in our own day, have culminated in the Welfare State : to them it was self-evident that society must evolve into a more liberal and open form, that ignorance must be put down and that social justice must be extended. The outward form of the Church must also change, in order to adapt itself to this new society; and Catholics must be prepared for a positive, open-handed policy of co-existence. When it was offered, it should be accepted with that degree of confidence and trust which one Englishman expects of another.

Unfortunately, the majority of those to whom this offer was made were Englishman only in name : in mental habits, education and instincts, they had more in common with the Roman Court and with the alien schools and seminaries in which they had been trained than with the England of Blue Books and Royal Commissions, of Gladstone and Arnold. To them Liberalism was what had happened to Pius IX in 1848, and they dwelt—so their critics among the converts believed—like the superseded gods in *Hyperion* :
"Deep in the shady sadness of a vale
Far sunken from the healthy breath of morn."
Their suspicions, nourished by timidity and ignorance, led

them to prefer the torpid security of the ghetto to the dangerous opportunities of Emancipation; and their fear of plain speaking encouraged them to believe that any concessions would precipitate disasters of apocalyptic proportions.

Even the most virile of them was infected, as first Simpson and then Newman were to discover. In a letter to Simpson on 8 March, Bishop Ullathorne had made it clear that the Bishops deemed it "absolutely unnecessary that the reasons for our own actions should be explained & that the Catholic community should be informed of the grounds of our proceedings"; and although he added "that the articles on the education question were not the exclusive grounds of the opinion formed of The Rambler by the Bps (Bishops)", he spoke severely of their author:

"As you mentioned to me that Bp. Turner had approved the first article in The Rambler, I ought perhaps to mention that I have received a letter from his Lordship, in which he says that so far from ever having done so, meeting Mr Stokes last Thursday, he expostulated with him, and showed him how injurious his course was to our cause, & how much the Bishops lamented it.

"My own Pastoral would have been very much stronger, and I should have pointed out the conduct of men, who placed in official relations with us, instead of communicating their sentiments officially (or at all events privately to us) had appealed to our flocks against us, before even ascertaining our motives; and my only reason for suppressing the strong portions of my Pastoral was the wish to avoid directly impinging on the Rambler articles."[1]

[1] From a Mss letter in the Downside Abbey Archives

In April, Simpson could not resist producing his own version of the affair in a long letter intended for publication in Montalambert's *Le Correspondant*.[1] It is passionate —the sense of injustice still burns strongly—and rather diffuse, and it seems not to have been published; but it has its insights. Simpson speaks of this "coup against the laity", in which "the English Hierarchy has been victorious; not over its enemies but over its friends; no new converts have been made, no enthusiasm excited, no burst of charity or zeal called forth by their artillery & their blows. They have triumphed over their own army, & have excited not the enthusiasm of Christian conquest, but the passions of civil war." He quotes a letter he has received from a most influential layman, a representative of one of the old Catholic families: "this whole story is a warning to all who by writing or public life of any kind wish to serve the cause of religion as independent laymen, or in any other quality or office than that of Bishops. If no other office is recognised, let us have it so declared. If all Catholic literature is to be confined to Bishops' Pastorals, and politics to be merely their echo, let it be known to all whom it may concern. If the dictum attributed to the Cardinal, 'the only function of the laity is to pay', be really the law of this land, let us know it, that we may get out of it into some more Christian country." Simpson comments that "this jealousy of the laity is a natural result of the strictness of the administrative organization which is now considered to constitute the strength of the clergy. . . . The compactness of the clerical union makes it a caste; it has a separate professional education and separate habits of thought. . . . The laity are to be

[1] Simpson

kept in ignorance of all religious questions except those in the catechism, in order to misuse their obedience to a body of directors professionally educated to manage their religion for them. Religion is turned into administration, the clergy into theological police, & the body of thinking laymen into a mass of *suspects,* supposed to be brooding on nothing but revolution, & only kept together by motives of fear, & by the external pressure of a clerical organisation."

The effect on British Protestant opinion of the Bishops' policy of non-co-operation over the Education question is, Simpson goes on to say, merely to arouse contempt. The question of religious education is no longer political but social, and can best be settled by negotiation, compromise and all the other arts that constitute the British political way of life: "we strive to make the stream run up hill again, and make it a political instead of, or as well as, a social difference".

It is important to remember that these observations were made before Newman's interview with Ullathorne. It was on 22 May that this famous meeting took place, at which Newman was told that even the May number of the *Rambler* was too disturbing for Catholic taste:

"There were remains of the old spirit. It was irritating. Our laity were a *peaceable* set; the Church was *peace.* They had a deep faith; they did not like to hear that anyone doubted."

Newman's record of the meeting continues: "I stated my own view strongly. ... he saw only one side, I another; that the Bishops etc., did not see the state of the laity, e.g. in Ireland, how unsettled, yet how docile.

"He said something like 'Who are the laity?' I answered

(not these words) that the Church would look foolish without them. He said, 'Could there not be an *Irish* Magazine?' I said, who was to conduct it?"[1]

In vain did Newman try to convince Ullathorne that the reason for his going to Ireland in the first place had been "the hope of doing something towards those various objects for which I had consented to undertake the *Rambler*. . . . He would not allow the weight of anything I said"; and when Newman reminded him of his initial unwillingness to take on the editorship, Ullathorne turned to him abruptly and said: "Why not give it up?"

It was agreed, in fairness to the proprietors and to Newman's own pocket, that he should give up the *Rambler* after the next (July) issue. There, "with no sort of unpleasantness", the conversation ended.

Newman's relief was tempered, as the news of his resignation circulated, by a growing sadness, and then by an increasingly familiar sense of frustration. Those converts who thought as he did regarded the event as a sign of the Bishops' inability to rise to the challenge of the times, and various exclamations of despair are recorded in letters to Newman:

"We must wait for a convert Bishop," wrote one correspondent; while another, H. W. Wilberforce, wrote: "I deeply feel that our Bishops do not understand England and the English. Either the Catholic laity will kick, or, what I rather fear, they will more and more fall below Protestants in intellectual training and have no influence on the public mind."[2]

[1] O.
[2] O.

Once again Newman felt that his mission had been repudiated. He tried to console himself with the reflection that "it may be God's will it should be done a hundred years later", but he could not hold back from the bitter reflection that "when I am gone it will be seen perhaps that persons stopped me from doing a *work* which I *might* have done". Again he felt obliged to defend himself against misinterpretation (a motive which, as the *Apologia* was to show in five years time, was always the most powerful to produce his best and most characteristic writing). This present essay is the result.

On Consulting the Faithful in Matters of Doctrine was published in the next and, for Newman, final number of the *Rambler;* and both its subject matter and style gain added significance when they are related to the background which has already been described.

It is clear from the way in which Newman links the *Rambler* issue with that of the Irish University and speaks of his particular mission that not only is the existence of a lively and educated laity fundamental to his conception of the Catholic Church and to his theology, but that the most fruitful approach to his work is to see it as a developed theology of the laity in all its ramifications. We are also able to see more exactly why Newman suffered as he did during his life in the Catholic Church, and why he suffered so deeply.

Only gradually and most unwillingly did he come to see that it was not his vocation within the Church to be as active as he had been when he was a tutor at Oriel. He was not to lead, to teach, to satisfy the needs of the laity; he was, rather, to suffer those needs, in order better to write about them; and he was to practise charity heroically that future generations of clergy and laity might be shamed into working together in a better spirit. Some eight years previously, in 1851, and before his Irish adventure he had referred to the laity as at all times "the measure of the Catholic spirit; they saved the Irish Church three centuries ago, and they betrayed the Church in England. Our rulers were true, our people were cowards". He was now to turn his attention to what appeared to be almost the reverse situation; and there is no doubt that he had been stung into this by the controversy over the *Rambler* and the spirit that it had manifested. What had scandalised him had been the attitude to the laity adopted, not merely by the Bishops, but by the one whom he most admired, Ullathorne. Even to him, a layman seemed, spiritually, to be a kind of "boy eternal", rather than a responsible adult partner, whose right it was to be consulted on matters within his competence; and it is this point which Newman chooses to subject to the strictest theological examination.

On Consulting the Faithful in Matters of Doctrine begins with what, at first sight, appears to be a rather donnish disquisition on the difference between the idiom of English and the theological use of Latin. In the latter sense "consult" means to take counsel with, but idiomatically the meaning includes ascertaining a matter of fact as well as asking a judgement. Thus consulting the faithful involves asking, as a matter of fact, what the belief of the faithful is, as a testimony of that apostolical tradition, on which alone any doctrine may be defined; and it was in this idiomatic sense (to consult the faithful, as we consult a body of evidence) that the word was used in the passage of the previous number of the *Rambler* to which objection had been taken. Newman reminds his readers, not without irony, that we cannot re-model our mother tongue, and reproves those, who desire that perfect technical accuracy of expression demanded in a Latin treatise, for jumping to the conclusion that its absence is a sign of self-will and undutifulness.

He now takes the offensive and asserts that even in the technical theological sense the laity have a right to be consulted, since the body of the faithful is one of the witnesses to the fact of revealed doctrine, because their consensus throughout Christendom is the voice of the Infallible Church.

Yet although at various times this consensus of the faithful can make up, for example, for the silence of the Fathers, infallibility is not, strictly, *in* that consensus, but rather the consensus is an indicium or instrumentum to us of the judgement of that Church which *is* infallible. Nevertheless, doctrines have been defined and determined at the request of the faithful—indeed, such deference has been paid to them, that their impatience has sometimes almost been feared; but this was always because such demands were the faithful reflections of the pastoral teaching, and the people were a mirror in which the Bishops saw themselves. Newman again permits himself an ironical aside when he adds: "I suppose a person may *consult* his glass, and in that way know many things about himself which he can learn in no other way."

Furthermore, the common accord of the faithful, of pop-

ulations and of nations, is—as St Augustine points out—
one of the chief factors which holds us, justly, within the
bosom of the Church; and "in matters whereupon the Scripture has not spoken clearly, the custom of the people of
God, or the institutions of our predecessors, are to be held
as law".

Newman concludes this part of his argument by sum-
marising the five characteristics of the consent of the faithful. It is to be regarded as a testimony to the fact of the
apostolical dogma; as a sort of instinct, *or phronema,* deep
in the bosom of the mystical body of Christ; as a direction
of the Holy Ghost; as an answer to its prayer; and as a
jealousy of error, which it at once feels as a scandal.

The second and fifth of these characteristics take us to
the heart of Newman's teaching. The *phronema,* that instinct deep within the mystical body of Christ, is obviously
a counterpart to the *phronesis* or illative sense which, in the
individual, is that power to make a real, as opposed to a
notional, assent in judgements of faith and conscience.

The fifth characteristic is related to Newman's justification of a liberal education: that what is true in a natural
sense can never be contrary to Revelation; and it is significant that he should quote the following passage from
Anglican Difficulties by way of elucidation: "it is the
property of life to be impatient of any foreign substance in
the body to which it belongs", since it was almost in these
words and from such attitudes that he was to base his case
for admitting Catholics as undergraduates at Oxford:
young men must be free to make mistakes in order to ac-
quire that real independence which gives vitality to the
spirit and, thereby, the power to expel error.

3

Newman now returns to consider in detail the evidences for the witness of the faithful during the Arian controversy. Theirs was the voice of tradition, and the Nicene dogma was maintained during the greater part of the fourth century not by the unswerving firmness of the Holy See, Councils or Bishops, but by this consensus fidelium. There was, therefore, a temporary suspense of the functions of the ecclesia docens, since the body of the Bishops in speaking variously, one against another, failed in their confession of the faith. Later in considering the details of the evidence, Newman remarks that the ecclesia docens is not at every time the active instrument of the Church's infallibility; by which he means that it may speak with divided voices or not at all, and then the consensus of the faithful constitutes an authentic instrument of the apostolic tradition.[1] What is certain is that, in the fourth century, such an absence of effective leadership caused laymen to express their sense of the truth that was within them in a way profoundly displeasing to those in authority.

Newman now turns to the evidence for the fidelity of the laity during the Arian heresy. He concludes by arguing that the consent of the faithful is one of those theological presuppositions of Catholic doctrine which become clear only when required for use, as for example when the contemplated definition of the Immaculate Conception was under discussion. He goes on to remark, with an irony which the events that precipitated his reflections richly justify, that although Arianism may not return and that

[1] v. p. 116[1] infra (footnote in 1871 text)

this age is one which can pre-eminently dispense with the testimony of the faithful, ("and perhaps this is why the consensus fidelium has, in the minds of many, fallen into the background"), yet each constituent portion of the Church has its proper functions, and no portion can be safely neglected.

Newman now enunciates the cardinal theological principle which he clearly felt to be involved, not merely in the historical question of Arianism, but in those unhappy controversies which had arisen as a result of his frustrated efforts to educate the laity and to see them established in the economy of the Church of his time:

"Though the laity be but the reflection or echo of the clergy in matters of faith, yet there is something in the 'pastorum and fidelium *conspiratio*', which is not in the pastors alone."

Devotion starts from below. Enthusiasm must be encouraged. The *ecclesia docens* is happier when she has enthusiastic partisans about her, "than when she cuts off the faithful from the study of her divine doctrines and the sympathy of her divine contemplations, and requires from them a *fides implicita* in her word, which in the educated classes will terminate in indifference, and in the poorer in superstition".

From his earliest Anglican days, Newman's emphasis had always been on the fullness of the Catholic idea; and in the Oxford University sermon which had anticipated the *Development of Christian Doctrine,* he speaks of that idea as the secret life of millions of faithful souls, of centuries passing without the formal expression of such truths, and of St Mary's keeping all these sayings in her heart and becoming thereby our pattern of faith, both in the reception and the study of Divine Truth.

It is the fullness of the Catholic idea which is testified to in the consent of the faithful, and this fullness can be mediated only through the metaphorical language appropriate to the formulations of religious dogma; but although there exists "a certain correspondence between the idea, though earthly, and its heavenly archetype, such that that idea belongs to the archetype, in a sense in which no other earthly idea belongs to it,"[1] the possibilities of misunderstanding are immense; and when our various attempts at scientific explanation and logical analysis end ultimately in some great impossibility or contradiction, we realise that the fullness of this reality can never be brought under the dominion of any single concept or any single method of explanation.

Under the pressure of inevitable change, heresies arise; and it is these which oblige the Church to define more positively the content and implications of the Revelation : thus arises that development of doctrine, which is "a more intimate apprehension, and a more lucid enunciation of the original dogma" by the Church. "But what is the Church as separate from pope, councils, bishops and faithful?"

The importance of On Consulting the Faithful is, as Professor Chadwick points out, that it is Newman's first attempt to resolve publicly one of the major difficulties in

[1] Oxford University Sermons, no. XV, para. 33

his theory of doctrinal development: how, before a definition, is the mind of the Church to be discovered?[1]

This contention is conclusively supported by the documents. On 21 July, 1859, Acton wrote to Simpson saying
that Newman was in great spirits at having the *Rambler;*
an article, "editorial as it appears, on the Education question", was being written by Newman for the next (May)
issue; and in July, says Acton, "he means to review Gillow".
Bishop's pencilled insertion against this sentence is: "Was
it in the *Consulting the Laity* paper that this idea issued?"[2]
Dr Gillow had just published a sixty-four page pamphlet
denouncing Döllinger's article in the *Rambler,* which had
attempted to provide the evidence and justification for a
statement by Acton in the *Rambler* for August 1858 that
St Augustine was the father of Jansenism. To Gillow's
rigidly syllogistic mind this meant that either St Augustine
taught Jansenism or he did not; and that if he did not, such
a proposition could be made only by a fool or a knave.
Since it was made with the backing of a theologian of
Döllinger's eminence, it was not a foolish utterance but one
arising from the worst motives; so it must be forcibly and
immediately denounced to Rome.

Such a mind, imprisoned within its black and white
logical categories, must have been quite incapable of understanding either the development of heresy or the development of doctrine; and Newman may have had it in mind to
give Gillow a history lesson upon the complexities which
inevitably attend upon the rise, flowering and suppression

[1] *From Bousset to Newman : the Idea of Doctrinal Development,* Owen
Chadwick, (Cambridge, 1957, p. 183).
[2] B. p. 70

of a particular heresy—in this case Arianism—and upon the
way in which the mind of the Church actually makes itself
manifest.

Döllinger had himself written to Newman on 26 May
asking whether he ought to reply to Gillow's pamphlet:
"You have thrown out bait in the Rambler to make me enter
into the ticklish question of the historical ignorance pre-
vailing in the common divinity of the schools."[1] But it
seems to have been felt that further intervention by
Döllinger would only increase the injury to the Rambler.

The unpublished correspondence between Newman and
Gillow, which is preserved at Birmingham Oratory, is
worth special consideration in this context, since it estab-
lishes even more precisely what Newman had in mind
when he was writing his article. Dr Gillow held the chair
of theology at Ushaw for twenty-three years, and at his
funeral in 1877 it was said of him that "the plain words of
scripture, the authoritative teaching of the Church, the infallible decisions of the Holy See, the testimony of reason,
the irresistible evidence of physical or mathematical
science—those alone satisfied his mind". He was a man of
parts—architect, chemist and inventor—but he had his
limitations: he was something of a crank: he invented a
watch, for example, by which he insisted on regulating the
College chronometer.

The correspondence begins on 12 May, when Gillow sent
Newman a copy of his answer to Döllinger and protested
against certain statements and principles in the previous
(May) Rambler, which "appear to me very objectionable".
He instanced especially the words: "If even in the prepa-

[1] O. 26 May, 1859

ration of a dogmatic definition the faithful are consulted, as lately in the instance of the Immaculate Conception."

Newman's reply on 13 May was curt and tart. He admitted responsibility for the passage objected to and asked for the objections to be more specifically stated. Of the policy of previous *Ramblers*, he said:

"I have had no more to do with the Magazine, directly or indirectly, before this number, than, I suppose, you have had."

Newman sent the correspondence to Ullathorne who, in his reply of 15 May, seems to side with Gillow as against Newman. Speaking of the Pontifical Letter (c.1848) referred to in the *Rambler* article, Ullathorne says:

"its sense was to invite each Bishop to ascertain the sentiments of his clergy, and, in prudent ways, the feelings of the laity, on the subject of the Immaculate Conception. . . . From the special injunction of prudence as to our mode of ascertaining the sense of the people, I understood that we were to ascertain that sense not from the people themselves, but from their pastors, who generally gave their proof from the devotions in use."

Speaking of the relation between the Church teaching and the Church taught, he goes on to say: "the impress can only be as the seal impressed, and if, having the seal, we find on it no signs of the impression it is supposed to have made, the impression must have come from another source."

Newman adopts the analogy of the seal and uses it, substantially modified, later on. Meanwhile Gillow was eager to continue the correspondence, and in his next letter (15 May) admitted to having read the May *Rambler* in the same

critical spirit as he had read the previous ones. Now that
he knew that Newman had become the editor, he professed
himself satisfied : right had triumphed over wrong, the
Bishops' control had been established, and the *Rambler's*
orthodoxy at last secured.

Yet he stuck to his guns. The offending phrase about
consulting the faithful implied "that the infallibility of the
Church resides in the Communitate fidelium, and not exclusively in the Ecclesia docente. Else the infallible portion
would consult the fallible with a view to guiding itself to
an infallible decision. But the above principle would be
characterised as at least *haeresi proxima*."

Newman replied by return on 16 May. He anticipates
many of the analogies (e.g. the barometer) used subse-
quently in the article, and objects to Gillow's view that the
infallibility of the Church is *exclusively* in the Ecclesia
docente :

"I understand Fr Perrone to say, on the contrary, that it
resides per modum unius in both, as a figure is contained
both on the seal and on the wax, and primarily in the mind
of the engraver."

In a further letter, dated 25 May, Newman asks Gillow
if he is not confusing the infallibility of the Church with
"the power and prerogative of definition" which alone belongs to the Ecclesia docens :

"It is very difficult to be quite accurate in one's wording
of scientific truth, even when one makes it a *point* to be
accurate. I can quite understand how you came to take my
*un*scientific and familiar word 'consult' in a theological
sense, as if it ascribed a 'judicium' to the consulted parties,
viz. because you are a theologian. The question is, whether

the ordinary English layman would have so understood the passage."

After the publication of the *Rambler* article in July, Gillow returned to the attack. In a letter of 28 August, he flatly contradicts Newman's claim that there could be a suspense of the functions of the Ecclesia docens, and asserts that a fides implicita is what the Church rightly demands. To assert otherwise would be "a caution to the faithful to be on their guard against the Church". Thus the tendency of the article might be "to induce speculative minds to think disparagingly of the infallibility of the Church, and to conceive that though the Church as a whole may be infallible, yet either of its parts, the Ecclesia docens or the Ecclesia discens may fail: or at all events, that if either of these parts be infallible, that infallibility does not reside with the Ecclesia docens but the Ecclesia discens. Thus they may be led to place the disciple above the Master. The step between this and placing the private judgement above the doctrinal authority of the Church is not a wide one.

"As I am conscious that I must attribute the appearance of this article to myself as having given occasion to it at least in some measure, I therefore deem it a duty to say this much of my impressions regarding it."

From Newman's notes on the original letter, it is clear that he at first meditated a brief but friendly reply; but after reflection he must have decided that in view of the length of Gillow's letter, he must once more try to teach him a more sensitive verbal discrimination. In his reply of 2 September, Newman protests that "suspense" did not mean "failure":

"I think it has a meaning far lighter even than 'suspension'. The 'body of bishops' was 'the actual mass at the time spoken of'—no more." As for the fides implicita, he repeats that "he merely speaks of the possibility of our inculcating on the faithful a sort of fides implicita which would terminate in the evils which he specifies".

But what really fires Newman is the rather easy way in which Gillow asserts that we differ from each other "materially in an important point of *principle*" :

"I do not think you can be aware of the force of your own words. Surely to use such terms to another on a point de fide, is a matter of grave offence"; and Newman had added in an unpublished draft of the letter :

"He who addresses another in these terms in a question of faith, begins where he ought to end. He forfeits the right of remonstrance and the hope of influence."

Gillow's reply of 16 September shows how little he is able to grasp the subtleties of Newman's reasonings or the force of his objections to the claim that they differed on principle. He protests :

"I did not say that we differ on a point *de fide*. For as regards the principle by which you regard the Church as a whole to be infallible *per modum unius,* I know not what it is : I could not therefore say that it is a point *de fide*. I asserted that consistently with what *I hold* as a matter *pertaining to faith,* it is impossible that there could be a temporary suspense of the functions of the *Ecclesia docens*. But *matters pertaining to faith* include not only what is *de fide* by an express dogmatic definition, but also the logical conclusions from that which is *de fide*."

After such a letter, Newman must obviously have felt

that it was fruitless to reply further; but as we shall see later, Gillow persisted in another quarter.

The implications of Newman's answer to his own question—how, before a definition, is the mind of the Church to be discovered—were quite obvious to his opponents. If the Church had a duty to consult the faithful, then it also had a duty to manifest itself fully as a conspiratio of priests and laity, as distinct from the existing practice of acquiescing in a laity which was either superstitious or indifferent, and capable of a merely notional assent in matters of faith.

His answer also led him to part company with Acton, whose preoccupation with the Church's political record had caused him to conceive the Church as co-terminous with the actions of its priestly officers, and conscience as that individualising faculty which was bound to collide with the inevitable consequences of unbridled priestly power. For Newman such a view allowed insufficiently for the limitations of the individual conscience, which could claim infallibility only in so far as it reflected the verdict of the whole world: "Securus judicat orbis terrarum" was what had brought him into the Church, and it lies at the heart of his conception of the consensus fidelium as the infallible voice of the Church. This is to see the Church under its mystical and not its political aspect, to see it as the mystical body saving *in spite of* the actions of its officers. It is clear that Newman sees the individual conscience (*phronesis*) as being fulfilled only in the *phronema*, or communal conscience of the whole Church: one was the mirror to the other, in which we could sometimes see ourselves more clearly, and by which our individual moral insights were fulfilled, completed and sustained. Under this, its mystical aspect, the Church is more than a political assemblage or aggregation of individual consciences: it is a real, because dynamic, community possessed of the therapeutic power which can quicken, purge and save the individual consciences of its members; and it alone is able to secure that associated sensibility—intellectual and spiritual —which is the secret of the whole, or holy, man.

Thus Newman was able to take in his stride not only the use and abuse of papal political power, but also the promulgation in 1870 of the doctrine of papal infallibility, since he saw that infallibility as the necessary means by which the mystical body could be kept in being as an actual existing community. Newman, therefore, saw the Pope as a ruler, not a philosopher: "he strangles whilst we prate"; and in his person the Church addressed the wild intellect of man with blows not words, adopting not the philosopher's pallium but the cope, broidered with mystic characters.

But amidst all his correspondence, meetings and misunderstandings with the chief actors in this tragedy of the higher Catholic journalism, Newman never denies their basic contention: that the nature of the opposition they encountered was itself a symptom of the Church's ill-health and mal-functioning. What he did insist on, at the risk of being labelled a sophist, was that this disease required a deeper and more theological analysis: it represented a demand for the fullness of the Church to be made manifest, for that fullness which is not in the priests alone, but only in the conspiratio of priests and faithful laity. This to Newman was the one thing needful; but it could be brought about only by means of concessions from both sides.

The laity must consent to be educated, and not resent the suggestion as an insult; but they must be educated in a special way, so that intellectual and spiritual growth took place at the same time and in the same place: the same spots and the same individuals must be at once oracles of philosophy and shrines of devotion.

But concessions must be made by the clergy. They must cease to practise a sort of spiritual apartheid and consent to work with the laity, and to find, for example, in a Catholic University "a middle station where clergy and laity can meet, so as to learn to understand and yield to each other, and from which, as from a common ground, they may act in union upon an age which is running headlong into infidelity". It was essential that the Church should teach the laity that the "obsequium" owed by them to religion was "rational"; but this could only be done if the laity were allowed more independence: the clergy must trust to life and to the power of what is living to eject what is false from its system.

This is not, however, to advocate licentiousness: it must be liberty under law. The liberty to make mistakes must be accompanied by the obligation to receive reproof when in error. Newman's vision is of a manly discipline: our privilege is to speak out, but Rome's duty is to speak back—equally warmly and equally definitely, since warmth and definiteness are required from both sides.

How very English all this sounds!

"We must have knocks. Ha! Must we not?"

Such sentiments were, however, more appropriate to Arnold's Rugby than to Wiseman's England; and it is no wonder that Newman, as he contemplated the ruins of his

Irish adventure and his attempt to save the *Rambler*, and began to plan the establishment of a church and house at Oxford, should say: "from first to last education has been my line".

The importance of *On Consulting the Faithful* is that it removes the argument from the realm of policy and discipline, and places it firmly within the context of theology; it has ceased to be a series of charges and counter-charges, of a dispute about the Bishops' behaviour over a particular question of educational co-operation, and has become an argument about the laity's place in the very heart, mind and structure of the Church.

That Newman was surprised by the reception his article received testifies to that simplicity of mind which his opponents, trained in a less scrupulous school, always persisted in mistaking for guile.

Ullathorne had written on 3 July to say that he thought that "the defender of the word 'consult' has not succeeded. . . . it was understood as intended in defence of laymen who had written on Theology in the Rambler. (&) was merely used, *more gladiatorio,* as an argument in defence of the Rambler's antecedents."[1] Citing Johnson's Dictionary, he went on to claim that the primary sense of the word both in English and Latin was "to take advice", and that Newman was using it in the figurative and secondary sense "to have regard to".

Manning's response is given in a letter, 22 September, whose moderate and sympathetic tone is particularly interesting in the light of later developments:

[1] O. 3 July, 1859

"our conversation in the Library about the article in the Rambler has been many times in my mind, and I wish you would write and print a sermon on the office of the Holy Ghost in the Church, in which you could bring out "in ordine theologico' what 'in ordine historico' as in the Rambler is confusing to common readers."[1]

The fire-eating Dr Gillow re-appears, this time joined with Bishop Brown of Newport, who wrote to the Secretary of Propaganda at Rome, Archbishop Bedini.[2] He begins by speaking of the disturbing influences of the Birmingham and London Oratories, which, filled as they are with converts rather than with "original Catholics", foster Protestant notions and feelings, "whilst a Catholic training of the mind, so essential to converts, can hardly be hoped for".

The *Rambler* article is then referred to, and the offending argument on pp. 75-77 infra related. Bishop Brown says that he had written to Dr Gillow suggesting "that he should publish a refutation of the statements of Dr Newman"; but Gillow had replied saying "he thought of replying to it, but was induced to retire from a course which ought to be taken by some one higher in authority; that he had written upon the subject to Newman, *receiving an unsatisfactory answer*".

"Perhaps the high authority of the Holy See is the best to deal with the case—It is most painful to see published by one whom we regarded (sic) as the best of our converts allegations and arguments . . . which might now seem to be the writing of a Calvinist."

[1] O. 22 September, 1859
[2] Newman's Delation. Some hitherto unpublished letters by the Rev Vincent F. Blehl, S.J., Dublin Review 486, Winter 1960-61, pp. 296-305

No reply was received, and the Bishop followed this letter up with another dated 30 October, in which not only does he refer to the objected propositions and proofs as "sophistical & dishonest", but he goes on to charge the argument of the final paragraph of the essay concerning the effects of a *fides implicita* with being "quite as bad as anything which went before it—in some respects, worse".

He includes an extract from a letter from Gillow, who refers to the article as "the most alarming Phenomenon of our times, & has made the old Catholics feel that they do not know where they can place their confidence. It has contributed to widen still more the division between the old Catholics and the Converts, which it appears to me the latter have been setting up ever since their reception into the one fold. They have a strong party . . . they have got into their hands the chief portion of the Catholic press, and if the breach continues to open as it is now doing, we shall see sad results."

In Bishop Brown's third letter the passages objected to are translated into Latin—it is ironical to remember that this was done in order to produce greater theological precision—since he translates the term "body of the bishops" as "corpus Episcoporum" and "general councils" as "Concilia Oecumenica": statements which taken in their *Latin* sense could indeed be said to border on heresy.

Propaganda took up the case, and at the end of the year, when Bishop Ullathorne was in Rome, he discussed the matter with Cardinal Barnabo, who produced Dr Brown's letters. The Cardinal pointed to the offending passages and remarked: "Ce n'est pas Sanscrit", whereby, says Ullathorne, "I understood him to mean that he perfectly understood the passages he was talking about". He added, "Le Pape est beaucoup peiné".

Ullathorne, at Barnabo's request, then undertook to bring the matter to Newman's attention, which he did immediately he returned to England in January 1860. In consultation with Ullathorne, Newman wrote on 17 January a letter to Wiseman, who was then at Rome, in which he asked for a list of the passages objected to, a copy of the translation in which they had been read by Cardinal Barnabo, and a statement of the dogmatic propositions which they were held to have infringed. In return Newman undertook to accept and profess such dogmatic propositions, to explain his argument in strict accordance with them, and to show that they were absolutely consistent with the English text.

Wiseman received the letter at a time when there were at least "twelve distinct matters connected with my own diocese or person, which must be treated or settled if possible before I leave Rome".[1] This letter not only makes it clear that he was weighed down by the strain of all these matters, but that he was, as he put it, unable to understand the full causes of the dispute:

"The late articles (in the *Rambler*) have given great pain, and Dr Ullathorne is charged with a mission of peace to Dr Newman. If he wished he would write an article explaining them rightly. I have spoken as well and as soothingly as possible. But I have not yet touched the general principles because I am in the dark."[2]

He adds, significantly, "This letter has greatly fatigued

[1] Cardinal Wiseman to Dr. Manning, 21 January (St. Agnes) 1860.
    Dublin Review, January 1923, p. 121
[2] *ibid.*

4

me." Wiseman, however, must have passed Newman's request to Propaganda, because he received on 30 January a schedule of those statements in the *Rambler* article to which objection was taken. He did not pass these over to Newman, and Newman heard nothing more until on 7 May he received a letter from Manning, in which the following passage occurred :

"The Cardinal desires his kind regards to you, and tells me to say that he has thought it better to wait till his return, when he hopes to bring the matter of your letter to a termination which will be acceptable to you."

Newman, however, heard nothing further from either Wiseman or Manning; and by June 1861 Rome had become impatient. Barnabo wrote to Ullathorne asking "if Fr Newman has complied with the promise, and what is your opinion about the recent things published in the *Rambler*".[1] It is very hard to understand why Newman was not enabled to make a direct answer there and then; instead we read that in the winter of 1862 Ullathorne was once more trying to "smooth things over" for Newman at Rome. Things were not brought satisfactorily to a head until the visit of Oratorian Fathers St John and Bittleston to Rome in the May of 1867.

"From that time," wrote Newman, "all sorts of suspicions and calumnies have attended my name. And, since we began the (Oratory) School, have both increased, and directed against it. ... I shrink from a society which is so unjust towards me."

The measure of his withdrawal can be seen from a memorandum made in 1874. Until 1859, the year of the *Rambler*

[1] Butler, vol. II, p. 319

controversy, he had written almost a book a year; from then until 1874, he wrote between three and four; and "the cause of my not writing from 1859 to 1864 was my failure with the *Rambler*. I thought I had got into a scrape, and it became me to be silent. So they thought at Rome, if Mgr Talbot is to be their spokesman, for, referring to the *Apologia* to Ambrose in 1867, he said of me : 'He had ceased writing, and a good riddance—why did he ever begin again.' I certainly had myself in 1860 anticipated his view in 1867 of my services to religion."

That Newman was not exaggerating can be seen from the letter written the same year by Talbot to Manning, concerning the address presented to Newman, signed by upwards of two hundred of the laity, led by the Duke of Norfolk, in which the phrase occurred : "We feel that every blow that touches you inflicts a wound upon the Catholic Church in this country." In his letter Talbot says that "if a check be not placed on the laity of England they will be the rulers of the Catholic Church in England instead of the Holy See and the Episcopate".

"It is perfectly *true* that a cloud has been hanging over Dr Newman" ever since the *Rambler* article, and that "none of his writings since have removed that cloud". Of the laity, Talbot goes on to say that "they are beginning to show the cloven hoof. . . . They are only putting into practice the doctrine taught by Dr Newman in his article in the *Rambler*." Talbot then asks his celebrated question : "What is the province of the laity? To hunt, to shoot, to entertain. These matters they understand, but to meddle with ecclesiastical matters they have no right at all, and this affair of Newman is a matter purely ecclesiastical. . . .

Dr Newman is the most dangerous man in England, and you will see that he will make use of the laity against your Grace."

In April 1867 Newman sent Fathers St John and Bittleston to Rome to discuss all the misunderstandings which had arisen over his plan to establish a house in Oxford: the purpose of the visit was primarily to vindicate Newman's orthodoxy and loyalty; and the matter of the *Rambler* article was soon introduced: "we both think," wrote Bittleston to Newman, "that our coming here has been of the greatest use in bringing out this rankling sore." On the advice of the Roman theologian, Perrone, it was agreed that Newman should, in writing of something else, take notice of the passages objected to and explain them; since it now transpired that the accusations against the article had been put in theological form by the Jesuit theologian, afterwards Cardinal, Franzelin in a lecture at the Roman College.

In 1871 Newman produced a third edition of *The Arians of the Fourth Century*, and he added to the appendix, as Note V, an abbreviated version of the *Rambler* article, together with a point by point refutation of Franzelin's objections; although the matter appears to have been settled to Rome's satisfaction by Father St John in 1867.

The changes in the version of 1871 are significant. The section dealing with the charge that there was a temporary suspense of the functions of the Ecclesia docens and that the body of the Bishops failed in their confession of the faith was meticulously revised, errors were corrected, references to the source material were inserted, and certain of the more controversial references were suppressed. Ref-

erences to St Basil's persecution and to his being treated
with suspicion and coldness by Pope Damasus are deleted,
so is St Hilary's charge that the ears of the laity were holier
than the hearts of the priests, as well as the assertion that
"the Ecclesia docens is not at every time the active instrument of the Church's infallibility".

The proofs of the fidelity of the laity were less drastic-
ally condensed, but errors were corrected, references to the
source material made more precise, some indications that
they were from English editions suppressed, and the italic-
ising of the more significant (and therefore inflammatory)
passages abandoned. Certain references to the turbulence
of the Roman people were cut out, but the most significant
deletion is that of a reference to the Arian persecution as
having nearly effected a union of certain Novatian and
Catholic churches, "for as they both held the same sentiments concerning the Divinity, and were subject to a
common persecution, the members of both Churches assembled and prayed together. The Catholics possessed no
houses of prayer, for the Arians had wrested them from
them".

The *Rambler* affair sank deep into Newman's mind, and
he drew two lessons of profound significance from it. The
first concerned the independence needed by Catholics,
priests and laity, in order to achieve that spiritual and
intellectual vitality which alone would protect them from
the spirit of the age and make the Church a fit place for the
reception of converts. Newman came to see that this independence would never come about as long as the régime of
Propaganda ruled the affairs of this country :

"This age of the Church is peculiar,—in former times, primitive or medieval, there was not the extreme centralization which now is in use. If a private theologian said anything free, another answered him. If the controversy grew, then it went to a Bishop, a theological faculty, or to some foreign University. The Holy See was but the court of ultimate appeal. *Now*, if I, as a private priest, put anything into print, Propaganda answers me at once. How can I fight with such a chain on my arm? It is like the Persians driven to fight under the lash. There was a true private judgement in the primitive and medieval schools,—there are no schools now, no private judgement (in the religious sense of the phrase), no freedom, that is, of opinion. That is, no exercise of the intellect. No. the system goes on by the tradition of the intellect of former times."

Simpson made the same point in 1859, but he had taken his analysis much further.[1] He attributed the change in the function and status respectively of clergy and laity especially to the French Revolution. Traditionally, the laity had been the protectors and advisers of the clergy, who had received an education abroad in pre-revolutionary times which had been the envy of the Protestants: "our priests brought back a tone and a manner which savoured of the salons of the Faubourg St Germain & an intelligence that might recal(l) Bossuet and Fénelon. They were *independent gentlemen. . . .* The strength which then mainly consisted in the force of individuals must now be sought in discipline & organization; a clergy of a different calibre, of different education, & different origin must make up for

[1] Simpson

individual want of weight by corporate union, by unques-
tioning obedience to absolute direction & by administrative unity."

A further consequence of the system was, as Newman
discovered, that matters requiring a theological attention
were evaluated diplomatically, in terms of their power to
cause good or bad "impressions", pain or pleasure; and the
penalty of defeat was no longer the precision of formal
condemnation, but the unending frustration of "life under
a cloud". In 1863, he had written: "And who is Propaganda? Virtually one sharp man of business, who works
day and night, and dispatches his work quick off, to the
East and the West."[1]

Ambrose St John's richly evocative portrait of the proceedings in Rome in 1867 at which Newman was "reha-
bilitated", and especially his portrait of the suave yet
ebullient Cardinal Barnabo, prefect of Propaganda, testify
to the consequences of such a jurisdiction, from which this
country was not released until 29 June, 1908. The past was
discussed in terms of whether or not in failing to attend
Manning's consecration breakfast, Newman had shown a
want of conformity to the Pope's mind; Barnabo's manner
would alternate between warmth and evasion: in one out-
burst of down-right heartiness, as St John calls it, he could
say: "I know Manning best, but I love Newman". His
secretary, Mgr Capalti, looked at matters in the same spirit,
and his solution to the question of how the Catholic members of the University of Oxford should be cared for was:
"let them have there a good priest to make their confessions
to, but not a man like Newman—that would be to encour-

[1] O. 13 January, 1863

age them". And when St John tried to get a word in edge-
wise, this is how the conversation ended:

"Then we are all agreed, and the whole thing can be
settled in two words—good bye—there is a Patriarch
waiting for me—*basta*—you will see the Cardinal tonight."

The consequences of the failure to distinguish between
the needs of diplomacy and theology caused Newman, once
again, to seek for the analogue of an existing situation in
the Early Church; and this produced his second and even
more significant lesson.

His discovery that the development of the Arian heresy
corresponded to the development of the Church of England
had contributed to his conversion; and he now thought that
he had detected the seeds of an earlier heresy, Novatianism,
in the behaviour of those who opposed his conception of
the fullness of the Church, which he believed it was the
purpose of his work to propagate:

"At present things are in appearance as effete, though in
a different way, thank God, as they were in the tenth century. We are sinking into a sort of Novatianism—the heresy
which the early Popes so strenuously resisted. Instead of
aiming at being a world-wide power, we are shrinking into
ourselves, narrowing the lines of communion, trembling at
freedom of thought, and using the language of despair and
dismay at the prospect before us, instead of, with the high
spirit of the warrior, going out conquering and to conquer."

Such a spirit was personified in Newman's erstwhile
disciple, W. G. Ward, the editor of the *Dublin Review* and
the foremost critic of Newman's methods and proposals for
educating the Catholic laity. In Ward, Newman felt that he
was experiencing all over again that narrowness and in-

tolerance of the worst kind of Evangelical Protestantism from which he had freed himself at Oxford:

"Pardon me if I say that you are making a Church within a Church, as the Novatians of old did within the Catholic pale, and as, outside the Catholic pale, the Evangelicals of the Establishment. As they talk of 'vital religion' and vital 'doctrines', and will not allow that their brethren 'know the Gospel', or are Gospel preachers, unless they profess the small shibboleths of their own sect, so you are doing your best to make a party in the Catholic Church, and in St Paul's words are dividing Christ by exalting your opinions into dogmas. ... I protest then again, not against your tenets, but against what I must call your schismatical spirit."

This narrowness, the very key-note of "provinciality"— as Matthew Arnold noted in his own analysis of the same spirit—had narrowed the Church down to a point where it was failing in its mandate to open itself to all men. Instead, it was producing people who dwelt in a small world and thought it to be a big one, who preferred the so-called "Catholic" atmosphere to the challenge of the world outside, and who—in failing to consult the laity or to allow for a true private judgement—were, in Newman's constantly reiterated words, "failing to prepare the Church for converts".

Newman's abiding vision was that, in the dark days that were approaching and have now inevitably come upon us, the fullness of the Catholic idea demanded that the intellectual layman become religious and the devout ecclesiastic intellectual. He had hoped that it was his vocation to

bring about the means by which this might be achieved—
by his University, his school, his house at Oxford, and his
support for the work of the *Rambler.* But it was not to be
so. His was that greater vocation still: to witness, by the
way in which he met and mastered the indifference, hosti-
lity, persecution and tardy recognition of his Catholic life
to the very embodiment of that ideal he had devoted his
life to foster: the practice of the saintly intellect.

In our disaffected century, when the established moral
currency is not formed by men of the stature of a Gladstone,
an Acton or an Arnold, but is the pale and superficial image
of a vanished conviction, that quality of saintly integrity
is of all things the most needful; and this, with a prevision
he shares with men like St Thomas More, Newman could
both see and feel, since the integrity of his mind is so deep
and so intense that he could experience an almost physical
revulsion from the injustice of a Talbot, and could kindle,
as in the case of Gillow, to a point of principle.

To examine many photographs of Newman is to learn
that as he grew older suffering entrenched itself upon his
features; and it was the suffering of one who had an essen-
tially and predominantly priestly, because Christ-like, de-
termination to save souls. His concern that the laity should
more fully participate in the fullness of the Church shows
him to be not less of a priest, but more so; and the sufferings
of 1859 were those of a shepherd held back from the salva-
tion of souls. Of him, in those months of recrimination and
counter recrimination, it can indeed be said, as of another
whom his critics have accused of thinking too precisely
upon the event:

"Now cracks a noble heart."

But it was a heart that could be fulfilled only in Him who is wholly fulfilled in all, in a conspiratio of priests and faithful people, and in a Church in which clergy and laity are determined to grow even more closely together, as witnesses, fully and without a thought for the consequences, to that light "shining like a lamp in some darkened room, until the dawn breaks, and the day star rises in your hearts".

JOHN COULSON

ON CONSULTING THE FAITHFUL IN MATTERS OF DOCTRINE

The Rambler
vol I, new series, Part II, July 1859, pp. 198-230.

The following text embodies the amendments made in 1871. In order to reconstruct the original *Rambler* text, include all words in [ ], omit all words in ⟨ ⟩, and ignore the footnotes.

ON CONSULTING THE FAITHFUL IN MATTERS OF DOCTRINE

A QUESTION has arisen among persons of theological knowledge and fair and candid minds, about the wording and the sense of a passage in the *Rambler* for May. It admits to my own mind of so clear and satisfactory an explanation, that I should think it unnecessary to intrude myself, an anonymous person, between the conductors and readers of this Magazine, except that, as in dogmatic works the replies made to objections often contain the richest matter, so here too, plain remarks on a plain subject may open to the minds of others profitable thoughts, which are more due to their own superior intelligence than to the very words of the writer.

The *Rambler,* then, has these words at p.122: "In the preparation of a dogmatic definition, the faithful are consulted, as lately in the instance of the Immaculate Conception." Now two questions bearing upon doctrine have been raised on this sentence, putting aside the question of fact as regards the particular instance cited, which must follow the decision on the doctrinal questions: viz. first, whether it can, with doctrinal correctness, be said that an *appeal* to the faithful is one of the preliminaries of a definition of doctrine; and secondly, granting that the faithful are taken into account, still, whether they can correctly be said to be *consulted*. I shall remark on both these points, and I shall begin with the second.

§1

Now doubtless, if a divine were expressing himself formally, and in Latin, he would not commonly speak of the laity being "consulted" among the preliminaries of a dogmatic definition, because the technical, or even scientific, meaning of the word "consult" is to "consult *with*," or to "take *counsel*." But the English word "consult," in its popular and ordinary use, is not so precise and narrow in its meaning; it is doubtless a word expressive of trust and deference, but not of submission. It includes the idea of inquiring into a matter of *fact*, as well as asking a judgment. Thus we talk of "consulting our barometer" about the weather : —the barometer only attests the *fact* of the state of the atmosphere. In like manner, we may consult a watch or a sun-dial about the time of day. A physician consults the pulse of his patient; but not in the same sense in which his patient consults *him*. It is but an index of the state of his health. Ecclesiastes says, "Qui *observat* ventum, non seminat;" we might translate it, "he who consults," without meaning that we ask the wind's opinion. This being considered, it was, I conceive, quite allowable for a writer, who was not teaching or treating theology, but, as it were, conversing, to say, as in the passage in question, "In the preparation of a dogmatic definition, the faithful are consulted." Doubtless their advice, their opinion, their judgment on the question of definition is not asked; but the matter of fact, viz. their belief, *is* sought for, as a testimony to that apostolical tradition, on which alone any doctrine whatsoever can be defined. In like manner, we may "consult" the liturgies or the rites of the Church; not that they speak, not that can take any part whatever in the definition, for they are documents or customs; but they are witnesses to the antiquity or universality of the doctrines which they contain, and about which they are "consulted".

And, in like manner, I certainly understood the writer in the *Rambler* to mean (and I think any lay reader might so understand him) that the *fidelium sensus* and *consensus* is a branch of evidence which it is natural or necessary for the Church to regard and consult, before she proceeds to any definition, from its intrinsic cogency; and by consequence, that it ever has been so regarded and consulted. And the writer's use of the word "opinion" in the foregoing sentence, and his omission of it in the sentence in question, seemed to show that, though the two cases put therein were analogous, they were not identical.

Having said as much as this, I go further, and maintain that the word "consulted," used as it was used, was in no respect unadvisable, except so far as it distressed any learned and good men, who identified it with the Latin. I might, indeed, even have defended the word as it was used, in the Latin sense of it. Regnier both uses it of the laity and explains it. "Cùm receptam apud populos traditionem *consulunt* et *sequuntur* Episcopi, non illos habent pro magistris et ducibus, &c." (*De Eccles. Christ.* p. i. §1, c. i., ed. Migne, col. 234) But in my bountifulness I will give up this use of the word as untheological; still I will maintain that the true theological sense is unknown to all *but* theologians. Accordingly, the use of it in the *Rambler* was in no sense dangerous to any lay reader, who, if he knows Latin, still is not called upon, in the structure of his religious ideas, to draw those careful lines and those fine distinctions, which in theology itself are the very means of anticipating and repelling heresy. The laity would not have a truer, or a clearer, or a different view of the doctrine itself, though the sentence had run, "in the preparation of a dogmatic decree, *regard* is had to the sense of the faithful;" or, "there is an *appeal* to the general voice of the faithful;" or, "*inquiry* is made into the belief of the Christian people;" or, "the definition is not made without a previous *reference* to what the faithful will think of it and say to it;" or though any other form of words had been used, stronger or weaker, expressive of the same general idea, viz. that *the sense of the faithful is not left out of the question* by the Holy See among the preliminary acts of defining a doctrine.

Now I shall go on presently to remark on the proposition itself which is conveyed in the words on which I have been commenting; here, however, I will first observe, that such misconceptions as I have been setting right will and must occur, from the nature of the case, whenever we speak on theological subjects in the vernacular; and if we do not use the vernacular, I do not see how the bulk of the Catholic people are to be catechised or taught at all. English has innovated on the Latin sense of its own Latin words; and if we are to speak according to the conditions of the language, and are to make ourselves intelligible to the multitude, we shall necessarily run the risk of startling those who are resolved to act as mere critics and scholastics in the process of popular instruction.

This divergence from a classical or ecclesiastical standard is a great inconvenience, I grant; but we cannot remodel our mother-tongue. *Crimen* does not properly mean *crime; amiable* does not yet convey the idea of *amabilis; compassio* is not *compassion; princeps* is not a *prince; disputatio* is not *a dispute; praevenire* is not *to prevent. Cicero imperator* is not *the Emperor Cicero; scriptor egregius* is not *an egregious writer; virgo singularis* is not *a singular virgin; retractare dicta* is not *to retract what he has said;* and, as we know from the sacred passage, *traducere* is not necessarily *to traduce.*

Now this is not merely sharp writing, for mistakes do in matter of fact occur not unfrequently from this imperfect correspondence between theological Latin and English; showing that readers of English are bound ever to bear in mind that they are not reading Latin, and that learned divines must ever exercise charity in their interpretations of vernacular religious teaching.

For instance, I know of certain English sermons which were translated into French by some French priests. They, good and friendly men, were surprised to find in these compositions such language as "weak evidence and strong evidence," and "insufficient, probably, demonstrative evidence;" they read that "some writers had depreciated the evidences of religion," and that "the last century, when love was cold, was an age of evidences." *Evidentia,* they said, meant that luminousness which attends on demonstration, conviction, certainty; how can it be more or less? how can it be unsatisfactory? how can a sane man disparage it? how can it be connected with religious coldness? The simple explanation of the difficulty was, that the writer was writing for his own people, and that in English "an evidence" is not *evidentia*.

Another instance. An excellent Italian religious, now gone to his reward, was reading a work of the same author; and he came upon a sentence to the effect, I think, that the doctrine of the Holy Trinity was to be held with "implicit" faith. He was perplexed and concerned. He thought the writer held that the Church did not explicitly teach, had not explicitly defined, the dogma; that is, he confused the English meaning of the word, according to which it is a sort of correlative to *imperative*, meaning simple, unconditional, absolute, with its sense in theology.

It is not so exactly apposite to refer,—yet I will refer,— to another instance, as supplying a general illustration of the point I am urging. It was in a third country that a lecturer spoke in terms of disparagement of "Natural Theology," on the ground of its deciding questions of revelation by reasonings from physical phenomena. It was objected to him, that *Naturalis Theologia* embraced *all* truths and arguments from natural reason bearing upon the Divine Being and Attributes. Certainly he would have been the last to depreciate what he had ever made the paramount preliminary science to Christian faith; but he spoke according to the sense of those to whom his words might come. He considered that in the Protestant school of Paley and other popular writers, the idea of Natural Theology had practically merged in a scientific view of the argument from Design.

Once more. Supposing a person were to ask me whether a friend, who has told me the fact in confidence, had written a certain book, and I were to answer, "Well, if he did, he certainly would tell *me*," and the inquirer went away satisfied that he did *not* write it,—I do not see that I have done any thing to incur the reproach of the English word "equivocation;" I have but adopted a mode of turning off a difficult question, to which any one may be obliged any day to have recourse. I am not speaking of spontaneous and gratuitous assertions, statements on solemn occasions, or answers to formal authorities. I am speaking of impertinent or unjustifiable questions; and I should like to know the man who thinks himself bound to say every thing to every one. Physicians evade the questions of sick persons about themselves; friends break bad news gradually, and with temporary concealments, to those whom it may shock. Parents shuffle with their children. Statesmen, ministers in Parliament, baffle adversaries in every possible way short of a direct infringement of veracity. When St. Athanasius saw that he was pursued on the Nile by the imperial officers, he turned round his boat and met them; when they came up to his party and hailed them, and asked whether they had seen any thing of Athanasius, Athanasius cried out, "O yes, he is not far from you:" and off the vessels went in different directions as swiftly as they could go, each boat on its own errand, the pursuer and the pursued. I do not see that there is in any of these instances what is expressed by the English word "equivocation;" but it *is* the *equivocatio* of a Latin treatise; and when Protestants hear that *aequivocamus sine scrupulo*, they are shocked at the notion of our "unscrupulous equivocation."

Now, in saying all this, I must not be supposed to be forgetful of the sacred and imperative duty of preserving with religious exactness all those theological terms which

are ecclesiastically recognised as portions of dogmatic statements, such as *Trinity, Person, Consubstantial, Nature,
Transubstantiation, Sacrament,* &c. It would be unpardon-
able for a Catholic to teach "justification by faith only,"
and say that he meant by "faith" *fides formata,* or "justification without works," and say that he meant by "works"
the works of the Jewish ritual; but granting all this fully,
still if our whole religious phraseology is, as a matter of
duty, to be modelled in strict conformity to theological
Latin, neither the poor nor children will understand us. I
have always fancied that to preachers great license was
allowed, not only in the wording, but even in the matter of
their discourses: they exaggerate and are rhetorical, and
they are understood *piè* as speaking *more praedicatorio.*
I have always fancied that, when Catholics were accused
of hyperbolical language towards the Blessed Virgin, it was
replied that devotion was not the measure of doctrine; nor
surely is the vernacular of a magazine writer. I do not see
that I am wrong in considering that a periodical, not
treating theology *ex professo,* but accidentally alluding to
an ecclesiastical act, commits no real offence if it uses an
unscientific word, since it speaks, not *more digladiatorio,*
but *colloquialiter.*

I shall conclude this head of my subject with allusion to a
passage in the history of St. Dionysius the Great, Bishop
of Alexandria, though it is beyond my purpose; but I like
to quote a saint whom, *multis nominibus* (not "with many
names, or "by many *nouns*"), I have always loved most of
all the Ante-Nicene Fathers. It relates to an attack which
was made on his orthodoxy; a very serious matter. Now I
know every one will be particular on his own special science

or pursuits. I am the last man to find fault with such particularity. Drill-sergeants think much of deportment; hard logicians come down with a sledge-hammer even on a Plato who does not happen to enumerate in his beautiful sentences all the argumentative considerations which go to make up his conclusion; scholars are horrified, as if with sensible pain, at the perpetration of a false quantity. I am far from ridiculing despising, or even undervaluing such precision; it is for the good of every art and science that it should have vigilant guardians. Nor am I comparing such precision (far from it) with that true religious zeal which leads theologians to keep the sacred Ark of the Covenant in every letter of its dogma, as a tremendous deposit for which they are responsible. In this curious sceptical world, such sensitiveness is the only human means by which the treasure of faith can be kept inviolate. There is a woe in Scripture against the unfaithful shepherd. We do not blame the watch-dog because he sometimes flies at the wrong person. I conceive the force, the peremptoriness, the sternness, with which the Holy See comes down upon the vagrant or the robber, trespassing upon the enclosure of revealed truth, is the only sufficient antagonist to the power and subtlety of the world, to imperial comprehensiveness, monarchical selfishness, nationalism, the liberalism of philosophy, the encroachments and usurpations of science. I grant, I maintain all this; and after this avowal, lest I be misunderstood, I venture to introduce my notice of St. Dionysius. He was accused on a far worse charge, and before a far more formidable tribunal, than commonly befalls a Catholic writer; for he was brought up before the Holy See on a denial of our Lord's divinity. He had been controverting with the Sabellians; and he was in consequence accused of the doctrine to which Arius afterwards gave his name, that is, of considering our Lord a creature. He says, writing in his defence, that when he urged his opponents with the argument that "a vine and a vine-dresser were not the same," neither, therefore, were the "Father and the Son," these were not the only illustrations that he made use of, nor those on which he dwelt, for he also spoke of "a root and a plant," "a fount and a stream," which are not only *distinct* from each other, but of one and the same *nature*. Then he adds, "But my accusers have no eyes to see this portion of my treatise; but they take up two little words detached from the context, and proceed to discharge them at me as pebbles from a sling."[1] If even a saint's words are not always precise enough to allow of being made a dogmatic text, much less are those of any modern periodical.

The conclusion I would draw from all I have been saying is this: Without deciding whether or not it is advisable to introduce points of theology into popular works, and especially whether it is advisable for laymen to do so, still, if this actually *is* done, we are not to expect in them that perfect accuracy of expression which is demanded in a Latin treatise or a lecture *ex cathedrâ;* and if there be a want of this exactness, we must not at once think it proceeds from self-will and undutifulness in the writers.

§2

Now I come to the *matter* of what the writer in the *Rambler* really said, putting aside the question of the

[1] Athan. de Sent. Dion. 8.

wording; and I begin by expressing my belief that, whatever he may be willing to admit on the score of theological Latinity in the use of the word "consult" when applied to the faithful, yet one thing he cannot deny, viz. that in using it, he implied, from the very force of the term, that they are treated by the Holy See, on occasions such as that specified, with attention and consideration.

Then follows the question, Why? and the answer is plain, viz. because the body of the faithful is one of the witnesses to the fact of the tradition of revealed doctrine, and because their *consensus* through Christendom is the voice of the Infallible Church.

I think I am right in saying that the tradition of the Apostles, committed to the whole Church in its various constituents and functions *per modum unius,* manifests itself variously at various times : sometimes by the mouth of the episocopacy, sometimes by the doctors, sometimes by the people, sometimes by liturgies, rites, ceremonies, and customs, by events, disputes, movements, and all those other phenomena which are comprised under the name of history. It follows that none of these channels of tradition may be treated with disrespect; granting at the same time fully, that the gift of discerning, discriminating, defining, promulgating, and enforcing any portion of that tradition resides solely in the *Ecclesia docens.*

One man will lay more stress on one aspect of doctrine, another on another; for myself, I am accustomed to lay great stress on the *consensus fidelium,* and I will say how it has to come about.

1.   It had long been to me a difficulty, that I could not find certain portions of the defined doctrine of the Church

in ecclesiastical writers. I was at Rome in the year 1847; and then I had the great advantage and honour of seeing Fathers Perrone and Passaglia, and having various conversations with them on this point. The point of difficulty was this, that up to the date of the definition of certain articles of doctrine respectively, there was so very deficient evidence from existing documents that Bishops, doctors, theologians, held them. I do not mean to say that I expressed my difficulty in this formal shape; but that what passed between us in such interviews as they were kind enough to give me, ran into or impinged upon this question. Nor would I ever dream of making them answerable for the impression which their answers made on me; but, speaking simply on my own responsibility, I should say that, while Father Passaglia seemed to maintain that the Ante-Nicene writers were clear in their testimonies in behalf (*e.g.*) of the doctrines of the Holy Trinity and Justification, expressly praising and making much of the Anglican Bishop Bull; Father Perrone, on the other hand, not speaking, indeed directly upon those particular doctrines, but rather on such as I will presently introduce in his own words, seemed to me to say *"transeat"* to the alleged fact which constituted the difficulty, and to lay a great stress on what he considered to be the *sensus* and *consensus fidelium,* as a compensation for whatever deficiency there might be of patristical testimony in behalf of various points of the Catholic dogma.

2.   I should have been led to fancy, perhaps, that he was shaping his remarks in the direction in which he considered he might be especially serviceable to myself, who had been accustomed to account for the (supposed) phenomena in

another way, had it not been for his work on the Immaculate Conception, which I read the next year with great
interest, and which was passing through the press when I
saw him. I am glad to have this opportunity of expressing
my gratitude and attachment to a venerable man, who
never grudged me his valuable time.

But now for his treatise, to which I have referred, so far
as it speaks of the *sensus fidelium,* and of its bearing upon the
doctrine, of which his work treats, and upon its definition.

(1.) He states the historical *fact* of such *sensus.* Speaking
of the "Ecclesiae sensus" on the subject, he says that,
though the liturgies of the Feast of the Conception "satis
apertè patefaciant quid Ecclesia antiquitùs de hoc senserit
argumento," yet it may be worth while to add some direct
remarks on the sense itself of the Church. Then he says,
"Ex duplici fonte eum colligi posse arbitramur, tum
scilicet ex pastorum, *tum ex fidelium* sese gerendi ratione"
(pp. 74, 75). Let it be observed, he not only joins together
the *pastores* and *fideles,* but contrasts them; I mean (for it
will bear on what is to follow), the "faithful" do not *include*
the "pastors."

(2.) Next he goes on to describe the relation of that *sensus fidelium* to the *sensus Ecclesiae.* He says, that to inquire
into the sense of the Church on any question, is nothing
else but to investigate towards which side of it she has more
inclined. And the "indicia et manifestationes hujus propen-
sionis" are her public acts, liturgies, feasts, prayers, "pastorum ac *fidelium* in unum veluti conspiratio" (p.101).
Again, at p. 109, joining together in one this twofold consent of pastors and people, he speaks of the "unanimis
pastorum ac *fidelium* consensio . . . per liturgias, per festa,

per euchologia, per fidei controversias, per conciones pate-facta."

(3.) These various "indicia" are also the *instrumenta traditionis,* and vary one with another in the evidence which they give in favour of particular doctrines; so that the strength of one makes up in a particular case for the deficiency of another, and the strength of the "sensus communis fidelium" can make up (*e.g.*) for the silence of the Fathers. "Istiusmodi instrumenta interdum simul con-junctè conspirare possunt ad traditionem aliquam apostoli-cam atque divinam patefaciendam, interdum vero seorsum. . . . Perperam nonnulli solent ad inficiandam traditionis alicujus existentiam urgere silentium Patrum . . . quid enim si silentium istud alio pacto . . . compensetur?" (p.139). He instances this from St. Irenaeus and Tertullian in the "Successio Episcoporum," who transmit the doctrines "tum activi operâ ministerii, tum usu et praxi, tum institutis ritibus . . . adeò ut catholica atque apostolica doctrina inoc-ulata . . . fuerit . . . communi Ecclesiae coetui" (p.142).

(4.) He then goes on to speak directly of the force of the "sensus fidelium," as distinct (not separate) from the teach-ing of their pastors. "*Praestantissimi* theologi maximam *probandi* vim huic communi sensui inesse *uno ore* fatentur. Etenim Canus, 'In quaestione fidei,' inquit, 'communis fidelis populi sensus haud levem facit fidem' " (p.143). He gives another passage from him in a note, which he intro-duces with the words, "Illud *praeclarè* addit;" what Canus adds is, "Quaero ex te, quando de rebus Christianae fidei inter nos contendimus, non de philosophae decretis, utrùm potius *quaerendum* est, quid philosophi atque ethnici, an quid homines Christiani, et *doctriná et fide* instituti, *sentiant?*" Now certainly "quaerere quid sentiant homines doctrinâ et fide instituti," though not asking advice, is an act implying not a little deference on the part of the persons addressing towards the parties addressed.

Father Perrone continues, "Gregorius verò de Valentiâ fusius vim ejusmodi fidelium consensus evolvit. 'Est enim,' inquit, "in *definitionibus fidei* habenda ratio, quoad fieri potest, consensûs fidelium.'" Here, again, "habere rationem," to have regard to, is an act of respect and consideration. However, Gregory continues, "Quoniam *et ii* sanè, quatenus *ex ipsis* constat Ecclesia, sic *Spiritu Sancto assistente,* divinas revelationes *integrè et purè conservant,* ut omnes illi quidem aberrare non possunt. . . . Illud solùm contendo : Si quando de re aliquâ *in materie religionis* controversia (controversâ?) constaret fidelium omnium concordem esse sententiam (solet autem id constare, vel ex ipsâ praxi alicujus cultûs communiter apud christianos populos receptâ, vel ex *scandalo et offensione communi,* quae opinione aliquâ oritur, &c.) meritò *posse et debere* Pontificem illâ *niti,* ut quae esset *Ecclesiae sententia infallibilis"* (p.144). Thus Gregory says that, in controversy about a matter of faith, the consent of all the faithful has such a force in the proof of this side or that, that the Supreme Pontiff *is able and ought* to *rest* upon it, as being the *judgment or sentiment* of the *infallible* Church. These are surely exceedingly strong words; not that I take them to mean strictly that infallibility is *in* the "consensus fidelium," but that that "consensus" is an *indicium* or *instrumentum* to us of the judgement of that Church which *is* infallible.

Father Perrone proceeds to quote from Petavius, who supplies us with the following striking admonition from St.

Paulinus, viz. "ut de omnium fidelium *ore pendeamus*, quia in omnem fidelem Spiritus Dei spirat."

Petavius speaks thus, as he quotes him (p.156): "*Movet me*, ut in eam (viz. piam) sententiam sim propensior, *communis maximus sensus fidelium omnium*." By "movet me" he means, that he *attends* to what the *coetus fidelium* says: this is certainly not passing over the *fideles*, but making much of them.

In a later part of his work (p.186), Father Perrone speaks of the "consensus fidelium" under the strong image of a *seal*. After mentioning various arguments in favour of the Immaculate Conception, such as the testimony of so many universities, religious bodies, theologians, &c., he continues, "Haec demum omnia firmissimo veluti *sigillo obsignat* totius christiani populi consensus."

(5.)   He proceeds to give several instances, in which the definition of doctrine was made in consequence of nothing else but the "sensus fidelium" and the "juge et vivum magisterium" of the Church.

For his meaning of the "juge et vivum magisterium Ecclesiae," he refers us to his *Praelectiones* (part ii. §2, c. ii.). In that passage I do not see that he defines the sense of the word; but I understand him to mean that high authoritative voice or act which is the Infallible Church's prerogative, inasmuch as she is the teacher of the nations; and which is a sufficient warrant to all men for a doctrine being true and being *de fide*, by the mere fact of its formally occurring. It is distinct from, and independent of, tradition, though never in fact separated from it. He says, "Fit ut traditio dogmatica identificetur cum ipsâ Ecclesiae doctrinâ, a quâ separari nequit; qua propter, *etsi documenta deficerent omnia*, solum hoc vivum et juge magisterium *satis esset* ad cognoscendam doctrinam divinitus traditam, habito praesertim respectu ad solennes Christi promissiones" (p.303).

This being understood, he speaks of several points of faith which have been determined and defined by the "magisterium" of the Church and, as to tradition, on the "consensus fidelium," prominently, if not solely.

The most remarkable of these is the "dogma de visione Dei beatificâ" possessed by souls after purgatory and before the day of judgment; a point which Protestants, availing themselves of the comment of the Benedictines of St. Maur upon St. Ambrose, are accustomed to urge in controversy. "Nemo est qui nesciat," says Father Perrone, "quot utriusque Ecclesiae, tum Graecae tum Latinae, Patres contrarium sensisse visi sunt" (p.147). He quotes in a note the words of the Benedictine editor, as follows: "Propemodum incredibile videri potest, quàm in eâ quaestione sancti Patres ab ipsis Apostolorum temporibus ad Gregorii XI. (Benedicti XII) pontificatum florentinumque concilium, hoc est toto quatuordecim seculorum spatio, incerti ac parùm constantes exstiterint." Father Perrone continues: "Certè quidem in Ecclesiâ non deerat quoad hunc fidei articulum divina traditio; alioquin nunquam is definiri potuisset: verùm non omnibus illa erat comperta; divina eloquia haud satis in re sunt conspicua; *Patres*, ut vidimus, in varias abierunt sententias; *liturgiae ipsae* non modicam prae se ferunt difficultatem. *His omnibus succurrit* juge Ecclesiae magisterium, *communis praeterea fidelium sensus;* qui altè adeò defixum ... habebant mentibus, purgatas animas statim ad Deum videndum eoque fruendum

admitti, ut non minimum eorum animi vel ex ipsâ contro-
versiâ fuerint *offensi*, quae sub Joanne XXII. agitabatur, et
cujus definitio *diu nimis protrahebatur.*" Now does not this
imply that the tradition, on which the definition was made,
was manifested in the *consensus fidelium* with a luminousness which the succession of Bishops, though many of them
were "Sancti Patres ab ipsis Apostolorum temporibus," did
not furnish? that the definition was delayed till the *fideles*
would bear the delay no longer? that it was made because
of them and for their sake, because of their strong feelings?
If so, surely, in plain English, most considerable deference
was paid to the "sensus fidelium;" their opinion and advice
indeed was not asked, but their testimony was taken, their
feelings consulted, their impatience, I had almost said,
feared.

In like manner, as regards the doctrine, though not the
definition, of the Immaculate Conception, he says, not
denying, of course, the availableness of the other "instrumenta traditionis" in this particular case, "Ratissimum est,
Christi fideles omnes circa hunc articulum unius esse animi,
idque ita, ut maximo afficerentur *scandalo,* si vel minima
de Immaculatâ Virginis Conceptione quaestio moveretur"
(p.156).

3.   A year had hardly passed from the appearance of Fr.
Perrone's book in England, when the Pope published his
Encyclical Letter. In it he asked the Bishops of the Catholic
world, "ut nobis significare velitis, quâ devotione vester
clerus *populusque fidelis* erga Immaculatae Virginis conceptionem sit animatus, et quo desiderio flagret, ut ejusmodi res ab apostolicâ sede decernatur;" that is, when it
came to the point to take measures for the definition of the

doctrine, he did lay a special stress on this particular preliminary, viz. the ascertainment of the feeling of the faithful both towards the doctrine and its definition; as the
Rambler stated in the passage out of which this argument has arisen. It seems to me important to keep this in
view, whatever becomes of the word "consulted," which,
I have already said, is not to be taken in its ordinary Latin
sense.

4. At length, in 1854, the definition took place, and the
Pope's Bull containing it made its appearance. In it the
Holy Father speaks as he had spoken in his Encyclical, viz.
that although he *already* knew the sentiments of the
Bishops, still he had wished to know the sentiments of the
people also : "*Quamvis* nobis ex receptis postulationibus de
definiendâ tandem aliquando Immaculatâ Virginis Conceptione *perspectus* esset plurimorum sociorum *Antistitum*
sensus, tamen Encyclicas literas, &c. ad omnes Ven. FF.
totius Catholici orbis sacrorum Antistites misimus, ut, ad-
hibitis ad Deum precibus, nobis scripto *etiam* significarent,
quae esset suorum *fidelium* erga Immaculatam Deiparae
Conceptionem pietas et devotio," &c. And when, before the
formal definition, he enumerates the various witnesses to
the apostolicity of the doctrine, he sets down "divina eloquia, veneranda traditio, perpetuus Ecclesiae sensus, singularis catholicorum Antistitum ac *fidelium* conspiratio. *Conspiratio;* the two, the Church teaching and the Church
taught, are put together, as one twofold testimony, illustrating each other, and never to be divided.

5. A year or two passed, and the Bishop of Birmingham
published his treatise on the doctrine. I close this portion
of my paper with an extract from his careful view of the

6

argument. "Nor should the universal conviction of pious
Catholics be passed over, as of small account in the general
argument; for that pious belief, and the devotion which
springs from it, are the *faithful reflection* of the pastoral
teaching" (p.172). Reflection; that is, the people are a
mirror, in which the Bishops see themselves. Well, I suppose a person may *consult* his glass, and in that way may
know things about himself which he can learn in no other
way. This is what Fr. Perrone above seems to say has sometimes actually been the case, as in the instance of the "beatifica visio" of the saints; at least he does not mention the
"*pastorum* ac fidelium *conspiratio*" in reviewing the
grounds of its definition, but simply the "juge Ecclesiae
magisterium" and the "communis fidelium sensus."

His lordship proceeds: "The more devout the faithful
grew, the more devoted they showed themselves towards
this mystery. And it is the devout who have the surest instinct in discerning the mysteries of which the Holy Spirit
breathes the grace through the Church, and who, with as
sure a tact, reject what is alien from her teaching. The
common accord of the faithful has weight much as an argument even with the most learned divines. St. Augustine
says, that amongst many things which most justly held him
in the bosom of the Catholic Church, was the 'accord of
populations and of nations.' In another work he says, 'It
seems that I have believed nothing but the confirmed
opinion and the exceedingly wide-spread report of populations and of nations.' Elsewhere he says: 'In matters whereupon the Scripture has not spoken clearly, the custom of the
people of God, or the institutions of our predecessors, are
to be held as law.' In the same spirit St. Jerome argues,

whilst defending the use of relics against Vigilantius: 'So the people of all the Churches who have gone out to meet holy relics, and have received them with so much joy, are to be accounted foolish' " (pp.172, 173).

And here I might come to an end; but, having got so far, I am induced, before concluding, to suggest an historical instance of the same great principle, which Father Perrone does not draw out.

§3

First, I will set down the various ways in which theologians put before us the bearing of the Consent of the faithful upon the manifestation of the tradition of the Church. Its *consensus* is to be regarded: 1. as a testimony to the fact of the apostolical dogma; 2. as a sort of instinct, or φρόνημα, deep in the bosom of the mystical body of Christ; 3. as a direction of the Holy Ghost; 4. as an answer to its prayer; 5. as a jealousy of error, which it at once feels as a scandal.

1. The first of these I need not enlarge upon, as it is illustrated in the foregoing passages from Father Perrone.

2. The second is explained in the well-known passages of Möhler's *Symbolique; e.g.* "L'esprit de Dieu, qui gouverne et vivifie L'Eglise, enfante dans l'homme, en s'unissant à lui, *un instinct,* un tact éminemment chrétien, qui le conduit à toute craie doctrine. . . . Ce sentiment commun, cette conscience de l'Eglise est la tradition dans le sens subjectif du mot. Qu'est-ce donc que la tradition considérée sous ce point de vue? C'est le sens chrétien existant dans l'Eglise, et transmis par l'Eglise; sens, toutefois, qu'on ne

peut séparer des vérités qu'il contient, puisqu'il est formé
de ces vérités et par ces vérités." Ap. Perrone, p.142.

3. Cardinal Fisher seems to speak of the third, as he is
quoted by Petavius, *De Incarn.* xiv. 2; that is, he speaks of
a custom imperceptibly gaining a position, "nullâ praecep-
torum vi, sed consensu quodam tacito tam populi quàm
cleri, quasi tacitis omnium suffragiis recepta fuit, prius-
quàm ullo conciliorum decreto legimus eam fuisse firma-
tam." And then he adds, "This custom has its birth *in that
people which is ruled by the Holy Ghost,*" &c.

4. Petavius speaks of a fourth aspect of it. "It is well
said by St. Augustine, that to the minds of individuals certain things are revealed by God, not only by extraordinary
means, as in visions, &c., but also in those usual ways,
according to which what is unknown to them is opened *in
answer to their prayer.* After this manner it is to be believed
that God has revealed to Christians the sinless Conception
of the Immaculate Virgin." *De Incarn.* xiv. 2, 11.

5. The fifth is enlarged upon in Dr. Newman's second
Lecture on Anglican Difficulties, from which I quote a
few lines: "We know that it is the property of life to be
impatient of any foreign substance in the body to which it
belongs. It will be sovereign in its own domain, and it con-
flicts with what it cannot assimilate into itself, and *is irritated and disordered* till it has expelled it. Such expulsion,
then, is emphatically a test of uncongeniality, for it shows
that the substance ejected, not only is not one with the
body that rejects it, but cannot be made one with it; that
its introduction is not only useless, or superfluous, or
adventitious, but that it is intolerable." Presently he continues: "The religious life of a people is of a certain quality

and direction, and these are tested by the mode in which it encounters the various opinions, customs, and institutions which are submitted to it. Drive a stake into a river's bed, and you will at once ascertain which way it is running, and at what speed; throw up even a straw upon the air, and you will see which way the wind blows; submit your heretical and Catholic principle to the action of the multitude, and you will be able to pronounce at once whether it is imbued with Catholic truth or with heretical falsehood." And then he proceeds to exemplify this by a passage in the history of Arianism, the very history which I intend now to take, as illustrative of the truth and importance of the thesis on which I am insisting.

It is not a little remarkable, that, though, historically speaking, the fourth century is the age of doctors, illustrated, as it was, by the saints Athanasius, Hilary, the two Gregories, Basil, Chrysostom, Ambrose, Jerome, and Augustine, and all of these saints bishops also, except one, nevertheless in that very day the divine tradition committed to the infallible Church was proclaimed and maintained far more by the faithful than by the Episcopate.

Here, of course, I must explain : —in saying this, then, undoubtedly I am not denying that the great body of the Bishops were in their internal belief orthodox; nor that there were numbers of clergy who stood by the laity, and acted as their centres and guides; nor that the laity actually received their faith, in the first instance, from the Bishops and clergy; nor that some portions of the laity were ignorant, and other portions at length corrupted by the Arian teachers, who got possession of the sees and ordained an heretical clergy;—but I mean still, that in that time of immense confusion the divine dogma of our Lord's divinity was proclaimed, enforced, maintained, and (humanly speaking) preserved, far more by the "Ecclesia docta" than by the "Ecclesia docens;" that the body of the episcopate was unfaithful to its commission, while the body of the laity was faithful to its baptism; that at one time the Pope, at other times the patriarchal, metropolitan, and other great sees, at other times general councils, said what they should not have said, or did what obscured and compromised revealed truth; while, on the other hand, it was the Christian people who, under Providence, were the ecclesiastical strength of Athanasius, Hilary, Eusebius of Vercellae, and other great solitary confessors, who would have failed without them.

I see, then, in the Arian history a palmary example of a state of the Church, during which, in order to know the tradition of the Apostles, we must have recourse to the faithful; for I fairly own, that if I go to writers, since I must adjust the letter of Justin, Clement, and Hippolytus with the Nicene Doctors, I get confused; and what revives and reinstates me, as far as history goes, is the faith of the people. For I argue that, unless they had been catechised, as St. Hilary says, in the orthodox faith from the time of their baptism, they never could have had that horror, which they show, of the heterodox Arian doctrine. Their voice, then, is the voice of tradition; and the instance comes to us with still greater emphasis, when we consider—1. that it occurs in the very beginning of the history of the "Ecclesia docens," for there can scarcely be said to be any history of her teaching till the age of martyrs was over; 2. that the doctrine in controversy was so momentous, being the very foundation of the Christian system; 3. that the state of controversy and disorder lasted over the long space of sixty years; and 4. that it involved serious persecutions, in life, limb, and property, to the faithful whose loyal perseverance decided it.

It seems, then, as striking an instance as I could take in fulfilment of Father Perrone's statement, that the voice of tradition may in certain cases express itself, not by Councils, nor Fathers, nor Bishops, but the "communis fidelium sensus."

I shall set down some authorities for the two points successively, which I have to enforce, viz. that the Nicene dogma was maintained during the greater part of the 4th century,

1. not by the unswerving firmness of the Holy See, Councils, or Bishops, but

2. by the "consensus fidelium."

I. On the one hand, then, I say, that there was a temporary suspense of the functions of the "Ecclesia docens." The body of Bishops failed in their confession of the faith. They spoke variously, one against another; there was nothing, after Nicaea, of firm, unvarying, consistent testimony, for nearly sixty years. There were untrustworthy Councils, unfaithful Bishops; there was weakness, fear of consequences, misguidance, delusion, hallucination, endless, hopeless, extending itself into nearly every corner of the Catholic Church. The comparatively few who remained faithful were discredited and driven into exile; the rest were either deceivers or were deceived.

1. A.D. 325. The great council of Nicaea, of 318 Bishops, chiefly from the eastern provinces of Christendom, under

the presidency of Hosius of Cordova, as the Pope's Legate. It was convoked against Arianism, which it once for all anathematized; and it inserted the formula of the "Consubstantial" into the Creed, with the view of establishing the fundamental dogma which Arianism impugned. It is the first Oecumenical Council, and recognised at the time its own authority as the voice of the infallible Church. It is so received by the *orbis terrarum* at this day.⟨A.D. 326. St. Athanasius, the great champion of the Homoüison, was elected Bishop of Alexandria.⟩

[The history of the Arian controversy, from its date, A.D. 325, to the date of the second Oecumenical Council, A.D. 381, is the history of the struggle through Christendom for the universal acceptance or the repudiation of the formula of the "Consubstantial."]

2. A.D. 334, 335. The synods of Caesarea and Tyre ⟨sixty Bishops⟩ against Athanasius, who was therein accused and formally condemned of rebellion, sedition, and ecclesiastical tyranny; of murder, sacrilege, and magic; deposed from his see, forbidden to set foot in Alexandria for life, and banished to Gaul. [Constantine confirmed the sentence.] ⟨Also, they received Arius into communion.⟩

3. A.D. 341. Council of Rome of fifty Bishops, attended by the exiles from Thrace, Syria, &c., by Athanasius, &c., in which Athanasius was pronounced innocent.

4. A.D. 341. Great Council of the Dedication at Antioch, attended by ninety or a hundred Bishops. The council ratified the proceedings of the councils of Caesarea and Tyre, and placed an Arian in the see of Athanasius. Then it proceeded to pass a dogmatic decree in reversal of the formula of the "Consubstantial." Four or five creeds, instead of the

Nicene, were successively adopted by the assembled fathers. [The first was a creed which they ascribed to Lucian, a martyr and saint of the preceding century, in whom the Arians always gloried as their master. The second was fuller and stronger in its language, and made more pretension to orthodoxy. The third was more feeble again. These three creeds][1] were circulated in the neighbourhood; but, as they wished to send one to Rome, they directed a fourth to be drawn up. This, too, apparently failed. [So little was known at the time of the real history of this synod and its creeds, that St. Hilary calls it "sanctorum synodus."]

5. A.D. 345. Council of the creed called Macrostich. This creed suppresses, as did the third, the word "substance." The eastern Bishops sent this to the Bishops of [the West][2], who rejected it.

6. A.D. 347. The great council of Sardica, attended by [380][3] Bishops. Before it commenced, the division between its members broke out on the question whether or not Athanasius should have a seat in it. In consequence, seventy-six retired to Philippopolis, on the Thracian side of Mount Haemus, and there excommunicated the Pope and the Sardican fathers. These seceders published a sixth confession of faith. The synod of Sardica, including Bishops from Italy, Gaul, Africa, Egypt, Cyprus, and Palestine, confirmed the act of the Roman council, and restored Athanasius and the other exiles to their sees. The synod of Philippopolis, on the contrary, sent letters to the civil

---

[1] These three creeds] Three of these
[2] the West] France
[3] 380] more than 300

magistrates of those cities, forbidding them to admit the exiles into them. The imperial power took part with the Sardican fathers, and Athanasius went back to Alexandria. 7. A.D. 351. [Before many years had run out, the great eastern party was up again.] ⟨The Bishops of the East met at Sirmium. The semi-Arian Bishops began to detach themselves from the Arians, and to form a separate party.⟩

Under pretence of putting down a kind of Sabellianism, they drew up a new creed, into which they introduced [certain inadvisable expressions][1] of some of the ante-Nicene writers, on the subject of our Lord's divinity, and dropped the word "substance." [St. Hilary thought this creed also Catholic; and other Catholic writers style its fathers "holy Bishops."]

[8. There is considerable confusion of dates here. Anyhow, there was a second Sirmian creed, in which the eastern party first came to a division among themselves. St. Hilary at length gives up these creeds as indefensible, and calls this one a "blasphemy." It is the first creed which criticises the words "substance," &c., as unscriptural. Some years afterwards this "blasphemia" seems to have been interpolated, and sent into the East in the name of Hosius. At a later date, there was a third Sirmian creed; and a second edition of it, with alterations, was published at Nice in Thrace.]

9. A.D. 353. The council of Arles.[2] [I cannot find how

---

[1] Certain inadvisable expressions] the language
[2] The Council of Arles ⟨The Pope sent to it several Bishops as legates. The Fathers of the Council, including the Pope's legate, Vincent, subscribed the condemnation of Athanasius. Paulinus, Bishop of Trêves, was nearly the only one who stood up for the Nicene faith and for Athanasius.⟩

many Bishops attended it. As the Pope sent several Bishops as legates, it must have been one of great importance. The Bishop of Arles was an Arian, and managed to seduce, or to force, a number of orthodox Bishops, including the Pope's legate, Vincent, to subscribe the condemnation of Athanasius. Paulinus, Bishop of Trêves, was nearly the only champion of the Nicene faith and of Athanasius.]He was accordingly banished into Phrygia, where he died.

10. A.D. 355. The council of Milan, of more than 300 Bishops of the West. Nearly all of them, subscribed the condemnation of Athanasius; whether they generally subscribed the heretical creed, which was brought forward, does not appear. The Pope's four legates remained firm, and St. Dionysius of Milan, who died an exile in Asia Minor. An Arian was put into his see. Saturninus, the Bishop of Arles, proceeded to hold a council at Beziers; and its fathers banished St. Hilary to Phrygia.

⟨A.D. 357-9. The Arians and Semi-Arians successively drew up fresh creeds at Sirmium.⟩

11. A.D. 357⟨-8.⟩ Hosius falls. "Constantius used such violence towards the old man, and confined him so straitly, that at last, broken by suffering, he was brought, though hardly, to hold communion with Valens and Ursacius (the Arian leaders), though he would not subscribe against Athanasius." Athan. *Arian. Hist.* 45.

12. ⟨And⟩ Liberius. A.D. 357 ⟨-8.⟩ "The tragedy was not ended in the lapse of Hosius, but in the evil which befell Liberius, the Roman Pontiff, it became far more dreadful and mournful, considering that he was Bishop of so great a city, and of the whole Catholic Church, and that he had so bravely resisted Constantius two years previously.

There is nothing, whether in the historians and holy fathers, or in his own letters, to prevent our coming to the conclusion, that Liberius communicated with the Arians, and confirmed the sentence passed against Athanasius; but he is not at all on that account to be called a heretic." Baron. Ann. 357, 38-45. Athanasius says: "Liberius, after he had been in banishment ⟨for⟩ two years, gave way, and from fear of threatened death was induced to subscribe." *Arian. Hist.* §41. St. Jerome says: "Liberius, taedio victus exilii, in haereticam pravitatem subscribens, Roman quasi victor intraverat." *Chron.* ⟨ed. Val. p.797⟩

13. A.D. 359. The great councils of Seleucia and Ariminum, being one bi-partite council, representing the East and West respectively. At Seleucia there were 150 Bishops, of which only the twelve or thirteen from Egypt were champions of the Nicene "Consubstantial." At Ariminum there were as many as 400 Bishops, who, worn out by the artifice of long delay on the part of the Arians, abandoned the "Consubstantial," and subscribed the ambiguous formula which the heretics had substituted for it.

[14. A.D. 361. The death of Constantius; the Catholic Bishops breathe again, and begin at once to remedy the miseries of the Church, though troubles were soon to break out anew.]

15. A.D. 362. State of the Church of Antioch at this time. There were four Bishops or communions of Antioch; first, the old succession and communion, which had possession before the Arian troubles; secondly, the Arian succession, which had lately conformed to orthodoxy in the person of Meletius; thirdly, the new Latin succession, lately created by Lucifer, whom some have thought the Pope's legate

there; and, fourthly, the new Arian succession, which was [begun][1] upon the recantation of Meletius. At length, as Arianism was brought under, the evil reduced itself to two ⟨Episcopal⟩ successions, that of Meletius and the Latin, which went on for many years, the West and Egypt holding communion with the latter, and the East with the former.

[16. A.D. 370-379. St. Basil was Bishop of Caesarea in Cappadocia through these years. The judgments formed about this great doctor in his lifetime show us vividly the extreme confusion which prevailed. He was accused by one party of being a follower of Apollinaris, and lost in consequence some of the sees over which he was metropolitan. He was accused by the monks in his friend Gregory's diocese of favouring the semi-Arians. He was accused by the Neocaesareans of inclining towards Arianism. And he was treated with suspicion and coldness by Pope Damasus].

17.   About A.D. 360, St. Hilary says: "I am not speaking of things foreign to my knowledge; I am not writing about what I am ignorant of; I have heard and I have seen the shortcomings of persons who are [present to][2] me, not of laymen ⟨merely⟩, but of Bishops. For, excepting the Bishop Eleusius and a few with him, for the most part the ten Asian provinces, within whose boundaries I am situate, are truly ignorant of God." ⟨De Syn. 63.⟩ It is observable, that even Eleusius, who is here spoken of as somewhat better than the rest, was a semi-Arian, according to Socrates, and even a persecutor of Catholics at Constantinople; and,

---

[1] begun] started
[2] present to] round about

according to Sozomen, one of those who [urged]¹ Pope
Liberius to give up the Nicene formula of the "Consubstantial." By the ten Asian provinces is meant the east and
south provinces of Asia Minor, pretty nearly as cut off by
a line passing from Cyzicus to Seleucia through Synnada.

18. A.D. 360. St. Gregory Nazianzen says, about this
date : "Surely the pastors have done foolishly; for, excepting
a very few, who, either on account of their insignificance
were passed over, or who by reason of their virtue resisted,
and who were to be left as a seed and root for the springing
up again and revival of Israel by the influences of the
Spirit, all temporised, only differing from each other in this,
that some succumbed earlier, and others later; some were
foremost champions and leaders in the impiety, and others
joined the second rank of the battle, being overcome by
fear, or by interest, or by flattery, or, what was the most
excusable, by their own ignorance." *Orat.* xxi. 24.

19. A.D. 363. About this time, St. Jerome says : "Nearly
all the churches in the whole world, under the pretence of
peace and the emperor, are polluted with the communion
of the Arians." *Chron.* Of the same date, that is, upon the
council of Ariminum, are his famous words, "Ingemuit totus
orbis et se esse Arianum miratus est." *In Lucif.* ⟨19.⟩ [That
is,] the Catholics of Christendom were surprised indeed to
find that [their rulers]² had made Arians of them.

[20. A.D. 364. And St. Hilary : "Up to this date, the only
cause why Christ's people is not murdered by the priests
of Anti-christ, with this deceit of impiety, is, that they
take the words which the heretics use, to denote the faith

¹ urged] were active in causing
² their rulers]the Council

which they themselves hold. Sanctiores aures plebis quàm corda sunt sacerdotum." *In Aux.* 6.]

21. St. Hilary speaks of the series of ecclesiastical councils of that time in the following well-known passage : ["It is most dangerous to us, and it is lamentable, that there are at present as many creeds as there are sentiments, and as many doctrines among us as dispositions, while we write creeds and explain them according to our fancy.] Since the Nicene council, we have done nothing but write the creed. While we fight about words, inquire about novelties, take advantage of ambiguities, criticise authors, fight on party questions, have difficulties in agreeing, and prepare to anathematise each other, there is scarce a man who belongs to Christ. Take, for instance, last year's creed, what alteration is there not in it already? First, we have the creed, which bids us not to use the Nicene 'consubstantial;' then comes another, which decrees and preaches it; next, the third, excuses the word 'substance,' as adopted by the fathers in their simplicity; lastly, the fourth, ⟨which⟩ instead of excusing, condemns. We [impose] [1] creeds by the year or by the month, we change our [minds about our own imposition of them, then] [2] we prohibit our changes, [then] we anathematise our prohibitions. Thus, we either condemn others in our own persons, or ourselves in the instance of others, and while we bite and devour one another, are like to be consumed one of another." ⟨Ad Const. ii. 4, 5.⟩

22. A.D. 382. St. Gregory writes : "If I must speak the truth, I feel disposed to shun every conference of Bishops; for never saw I synod brought to a happy issue, and

[1] impose] determine
[2] minds about . . . of them, then] own determinations,

remedying, and not rather aggravating, existing evils. For rivalry and ambition are stronger than reason, —do not think me extravagant for saying so, —and a mediator is more likely to incur some imputation himself than to clear up the imputations which others lie under." *Ep.* 129. [It must ever be kept in mind that a passage like this only relates, and is here quoted as only relating, to that miserable time of which it is spoken. Nothing more can be argued from it that that the "Ecclesia docens" is not at every time the active instrument of the Church's infallibility.]

II.   Now we come secondly to the proofs of the fidelity of the laity, and the effectiveness of that fidelity, during that domination of imperial heresy to which the foregoing passages have related. I have abridged the extracts which follow, but not, I hope, to the injury of their sense.

1.   ALEXANDRIA. "We suppose," says Athanasius, "you are not ignorant what outrages they (the Arian Bishops) committed at Alexandria, for they are reported everywhere. They attacked the *holy virgins and brethren* with naked swords; they beat with scourges their persons, esteemed honourable in God's sight, so that their feet were lamed by the stripes, whose souls were whole and sound in purity and all good works." Athan. *Op. c. Arian.* 15, [Oxf: tr.]

"Accordingly Constantius writes letters, and commences *a persecution against all.* Gathering together a multitude of herdsmen and shepherds, and dissolute youths belonging to the town, armed with swords and clubs, they attacked in a body *the Church* of Quirinus : and *some* they slew, *some* they trampled under foot, *others* they beat with stripes and cast into prison or banished. They hauled away many *women* also, and dragged them openly into the court, and insulted them, dragging them by the hair. *Some* they proscribed; from *some* they took away their bread, for no other reason but that they might be induced to join the Arians, and receive Gregory (the Arian Bishop), who had been sent by the Emperor." Athan. *Hist. Arian.* §10.

"On the week that succeeded the holy Pentecost, when the *people,* after their fast, had gone out to the cemetery to pray, because that *all* refused communion with George (the Arian Bishop), the commander, Sebastian, straightway with a multitude of soldiers proceeded to *attack the people,* though it was the Lord's day; and finding a few praying, (for the greater part had already retired on account of the lateness of the hour,) having lighted a pile, he placed certain *virgins* near the fire, and endeavoured to force them to say that they were of the Arian faith. And having seized on *forty men,* he cut some fresh twigs of the palm-tree, with the thorns upon them, and scourged them on the back so severely that some of them were for a long time under medical treatment, on account of the thorns which had entered their flesh, and others, unable to bear up under their sufferings, died. All those whom they had taken, both the men and the virgins, they sent away into banishment to the great oasis. Moreover, they immediately banished out of Egypt and Libya the following Bishops (sixteen), and the presbyters, Hierax and Dioscorus: some of them died on the way, others in the place of their banishment. They caused also more than thirty Bishops to take to flight." *Apol. de Fug.* 7.

2. EGYPT. "The Emperor Valens having issued an edict commanding that the orthodox should be expelled

7

both from Alexandria and the rest of Egypt, *depopulation and ruin to an immense extent immediately followed; some* were dragged before the tribunals, others cast into prison, and many tortured in various ways; all sorts of punishment being inflicted upon persons who aimed only at peace and quiet." Socr. *Hist.* iv. 24, [Bohn.]

3.   THE MONKS OF EGYPT. "*Antony left the solitude* of the desert to go about every part of the city (Alexandria), warning the inhabitants that the Arians were opposing the truth, and that the doctrines of the Apostles were preached only by Athanasius." Theod. *Hist.* iv. 27, [Bohn.]

"Lucius, the Arian, with a considerable body of troops, proceeded to the *monasteries* of Egypt, where he in person assailed the assemblage of holy men with greater fury than the ruthless soldiery. When these excellent persons remained unmoved by all the violence, in despair he advised the military chief to send the fathers of the monks, the Egyptian Macarius and his namesake of Alexandria, into exile." Socr. iv. 24.

OF CONSTANTINOPLE. "*Isaac*, on seeing the emperor depart at the head of his army, exclaimed, 'You who have declared war against God cannot gain His aid. Cease from fighting against Him, and He will terminate the war. Restore the pastors to their flocks, and then you will obtain a bloodless victory." [*Ibid*[1] 34.]

OF SYRIA, &c. "That these heretical doctrines (Apollinarian and Eunomian) did not finally become predominant is *mainly to be attributed to the zeal of the monks* of this period; for *all the monks* of Syria, Cappadocia, and the neighbouring provinces *were sincerely attached to the*

[1] ibid. 34] Theod. iv.

Nicene faith. The same fate awaited them which had been experienced by the Arians; for they incurred the full weight of the popular odium and aversion, when it was observed that their sentiments were regarded with suspicion, by the monks." Sozom. [*Hist.* vii.][1] 27, [Bohn.]

OF CAPPADOCIA. "Gregory, the father of Gregory Theologus, otherwise a most excellent man and a zealous defender of the true and Catholic religion, not being on his guard against the artifices of the Arians, such was his simplicity, received with kindness certain men who were contaminated with the poison, and subscribed an impious proposition of theirs. This moved the monks to such indignation, that they *withdrew forthwith from his communion,* and took with them, after their example, *a considerable part of his flock.*" Ed. Bened. *Monit. in Greg. Naz.* Orat. 6.

[4. SYRIA. "Syria and the neighbouring provinces were plunged into confusion and disorder, for the Arians were very numerous in these parts, and had possession of the churches. The members of the Catholic Church *were not,* however, *few in numbers.* It was through their instrumentality that the Church of Antioch was preserved from the encroachments of the Arians, and enabled to resist the power of Valens. Indeed, it appears that all the Churches which were governed by men who were firmly attached to the faith did not deviate from the form of doctrine which they had originally embraced." Sozom. vi. 21]

5. ANTIOCH. "Whereas he (the Bishop Leontius) took part in the blasphemy of Arius, he made a point of concealing this disease, partly *for fear of the multitude,* partly for the menaces of Constantius; so those who

[1] Hist. vii] vi

followed the apostolical dogmas gained from him neither
patronage nor ordination, but those who held Arianism were
allowed the fullest liberty of speech, and were placed in the
ranks of the sacred ministry. But Flavian and Diodorus,
who had embraced the ascetical life, and maintained the
apostolical dogmas, *openly withstood* Leontius's machina-
tions against religious doctrine. They threatened that they
would retire from the communion of his Church, and would
go to the West, and reveal his intrigues. Though they were
not as yet in the sacred ministry, but were *in the ranks of
the laity,* night and day they used to excite all the people to
zeal for religion. They were the first to divide the singers
into two choirs, and to teach them to sing [alternately][1] the
strains of David. They too, assembling the devout at the
shrines of the martyrs, passed the whole night there in
hymns to God. These things Leontius seeing, did not think
it safe to hinder them, for he saw that *the multitude was
especially well affected* towards those excellent persons.
Nothing, however, could persuade Leontius to correct his
wickedness. It follows, that among the clergy were many
who were infected with the heresy: but *the mass of the
people were champions of orthodoxy.*" Theodor. *Hist.* ii. 24.

6.   EDESSA. "There is in that city a magnificent church,
dedicated to St. Thomas the Apostle, wherein, on account
of the sanctity of the place, religious assemblies are con-
tinually held. The Emperor Valens wished to inspect this
edifice; when, having learned that *all who usually congre-
gated there were opposed to the heresy* which he favoured,
he is said to have struck the prefect with his own hand, because he had neglected to expel them thence. The prefect,

[1] alternately] in alternate parts

to prevent the slaughter of *so great a number* of persons, privately warned them against resorting thither. But his admonitions and menaces were alike unheeded; for on the following day *they all crowded to the church.* When the prefect was going towards it with a large military force, a poor woman, leading her own little child by the hand, hurried hastily by on her way to the church, breaking through the ranks of the soldiery. The prefect, irritated at this, ordered her to be brought to him, and thus addressed her: 'Wretched woman, whither are you running in so disorderly a manner?' She replied, 'To the same place that others are hastening.' 'Have you not heard,' said he, 'that the prefect is about to put to death all that shall be found there?' 'Yes,' said the woman, 'and therefore I hasten, that I may be found there.' 'And whither are you dragging that little child?' said the prefect. The woman answered, *'That he also may be vouchsafed the honour of martyrdom.'* The prefect went back and informed the emperor that *all were ready to die in behalf of their own faith;* and added that it would be preposterous to destroy so many persons at one time, and thus succeeded in restraining the emperor's wrath." Socr. iv. 18. "Thus was the Christian faith confessed by the *whole city* of Edessa." Sozom. vi. 18.

7. SAMOSATA. "The Arians, having deprived this exemplary flock of their shepherd, elected in his place an individual with whom *none of the inhabitants of the city,* whether poor or rich, servants or mechanics, husbandmen or gardeners, men or women, young or old, would hold communion. *He was left quite alone;* no one even calling to see him, or exchanging a word with him. It is, however,

said that his disposition was extremely gentle; and this is proved by what I am about to relate. One day, when he went to bathe in the public baths, the attendants closed the doors; but he ordered the doors to be thrown open, that the people might be admitted to bathe with himself. Perceiving that they remained in a standing posture before him, imagining that great deference towards himself was the cause of this conduct, he arose and left the bath. *These people believed that the water had been contaminated by his heresy,* and ordered it to be let out and fresh water to be supplied. When he heard of this circumstance, he left the city, thinking that he ought no longer to remain in a place *where he was the object of public aversion and hatred.* Upon this retirement of Eunomius, Lucius was elected as his successor by the Arians. Some young persons were amusing themselves with playing at ball in the market-place; Lucius was passing by at the time, and the ball happened to fall beneath the feet of the ass on which he was mounted. *The youths uttered loud exclamations, believing that the ball was contaminated.* They lighted a fire, and hurled the ball through it, believing that by this process the ball would be purified. Although this was only a childish deed, and although it exhibits the remains of ancient superstition, yet it is *sufficient to show the odium which the Arian faction had incurred in this city.* Lucius was far from imitating the mildness of Eunomius, and he persuaded the heads of government to exile most of the clergy." Theodor. iv. 15.

8.   OSRHOENE. "Arianism met with similar opposition at the same period in Osrhoëne and Cappadocia. Basil, Bishop of Caesarea, and Gregory, Bishop of Nazianzus,

were held in high admiration and esteem *throughout these regions.*" Sozom. vi. 21.

9. CAPPADOCIA. "Valens, in passing through Cappadocia, did all in his power to injure the orthodox, and to deliver up the churches to the Arians. He thought to accomplish his designs more easily on account of a dispute which was then pending between Basil and Eusebius, who governed the Church of Caesarea. This dissension had been the cause of Basil's departing to Pontus. *The people, and some of the most powerful and wisest men of the city,* began to regard Eusebius with suspicion, and to meditate a secession from his communion. The emperor and the Arian Bishops regarded the absence of Basil, and the hatred of the people towards Eusebius, as circumstances that would tend greatly to the success of their designs. *But their expectations were utterly frustrated.* On the first intelligence of the intention of the emperor to pass through Cappadocia, Basil returned to Caesarea, where he effected a reconciliation with Eusebius. The projects of Valens were thus defeated, and he returned with his Bishops." Sozom. vi. 15.

10. PONTUS. "It is said that when Eulalius, Bishop of Amasia in Pontus, returned from exile, he found that his Church had passed into the hands of an Arian, and that *scarcely fifty inhabitants of the city* had submitted to the control of their new Bishop." Sozom. vii. 2.

11. ARMENIA. "That company of Arians, who came with Eustathius to Nicopolis, had promised that they would bring over this city to compliance with the commands of the imperial vicar. This city had great ecclesiastical importance, both because it was the metropolis of Armenia, and because it had been ennobled by the blood of martyrs, and

governed hitherto by Bishops of great reputation, and thus, as Basil calls it, was the nurse of religion and the metropolis of sound doctrine. Fronto, one of the city presbyters, who had hitherto shown himself as a champion of the truth, through ambition gave himself up to the enemies of Christ, and purchased the bishopric of the Arians at the price of renouncing the Catholic faith. This wicked proceeding of Eustathius and the Arians brought a new glory instead of evil to the Nicopolitans, since it gave them an opportunity of defending the faith. Fronto, indeed, the Arians consecrated, *but there was a remarkable unanimity of clergy and people in rejecting him.* Scarcely one or two clerks sided with him; on the contrary, he *became the execration of all Armenia.*" *Vita S. Basil.,* Bened. pp. clvii, clviii.

12.   NICOMEDIA. "Eighty pious clergy proceeded to Nicomedia, and there presented to the emperor a supplicatory petition complaining of the ill-usage to which they had been subjected. Valens, dissembling his displeasure in their presence, gave Modestus, the prefect, a secret order to apprehend these persons and put them to death. The prefect, *fearing that he should excite the populace to a seditious movement* against himself, if he attempted the public execution of so many, pretended to send them away into exile," &c. Socr. iv. 16.

13.   [ASIA MINOR.][1] St. Basil says, about the year 372: "Religious people keep silence, but every blaspheming tongue is let loose. Sacred things are profaned; *those of the laity* who are sound in faith *avoid the places of worship* as schools of impiety, and raise their hands in solitude, with groans and tears, to the Lord in heaven." *Ep.* 92. Four

[1] ASIA MINOR] CAPPADOCIA

years after he writes : "Matters have come to this pass; *the people have left their houses of prayer,* and assemble in deserts: a pitiable sight; *women and children, old men, and [others]¹ infirm,* wretchedly faring in the open air, amid the most profuse rains and snow-storms, and winds, and frost⟨s⟩ of winter; and again in summer under a scorching sun. To this they submit, because they *will have no part in the wicked Arian leaven."* Ep. 242. Again : "Only one offence is now vigorously punished, an accurate observance of our fathers' traditions. For this cause the pious are driven from their countries, and transported into deserts. The *people are in lamentation,* in continual tears at home and abroad. There is a cry in the city, a cry in the country, in the roads, in the deserts. Joy and spiritual cheerfulness are no more; our feasts are turned into mourning; our houses of prayer are shut up, our altars deprived of the spiritual worship." Ep. 243.

⟨PAPHLAGONIA, &c. "I thought," says Julian in one of his Epistles, "that the leaders of the Galilaeans would feel more grateful to me than to my predecessor. For in his time they were in great numbers turned out of their homes, and persecuted, and imprisoned; moreover, multitudes of so-called heretics" (the Novatians who were with the Catholics against the Arians) "were slaughtered, so that in Samosata, Paphlagonia, Bithynia, and Galatia, and many other nations, villages were utterly sacked and destroyed." Ep. 52.⟩

14.   SCYTHIA. "There are in this country a great number of cities, of towns, and of fortresses. According to an ancient custom which still prevails, all the churches of

¹ others] men otherwise

the whole country are under the sway of one Bishop. Valens (the emperor) repaired to the church, and strove to gain over the Bishop to the heresy of Arius; but this latter manfully opposed his arguments, and, after a courageous defence of the Nicene doctrines, quitted the emperor, and proceeded to another church, *whither he was followed by the people. Valens was extremely offended at being left alone* in a church with his attendants, and, in resentment, condemned Vetranio (the Bishop) to banishment. Not long after, however, he recalled him, because, I believe, *he apprehended an insurrection."* Sozom. vi. 21.

15.   CONSTANTINOPLE. "Those who acknowledged the doctrine of consubstantiality were not only expelled from the churches, but also from the cities. But although expulsion at first satisfied them (the Arians), they soon proceeded to the worse extremity of inducing compulsory communion with them, caring little for such a desecration of the churches. They resorted to all kinds of scourgings, a variety of tortures, and confiscation of property. Many were punished with exile, some died under the torture, and others were put to death while being driven from their country. *These atrocities were exercised throughout all the eastern cities*, but especially at Constantinople." Socr ii. 27.

[The following passage is quoted for the substantial fact which it contains, viz. the testimony of popular tradition to the Catholic doctrine: "At this period a union was nearly effected between the Novatian and Catholic Churches; for, as they both *held the same sentiments concerning the Divinity*, and were subjected to a common persecution, the members of both Churches assembled and prayed together. The Catholics then possessed no houses of prayer, for the Arians had wrested them from them." Sozom. iv 20.]

16. ILLYRIA. "The parents of Theodosius were Christians, and were attached to the Nicene doctrine, hence he took pleasure in the ministration of Ascholius (Bishop of Thessalonica). He also rejoiced at finding that the *Arian heresy had not been received in Illyria.*" Sozom. vii. 4.

17. NEIGHBOURHOOD OF MACEDONIA. "Theodosius inquired concerning the religious sentiments which were prevalent in the other provinces, and ascertained that, as far as Macedonia, *one form of belief was universally predominant,*" &c. Ibid.

18. ROME. "With respect to doctrine no dissension arose either at Rome or in any other of the Western Churches. *The people unanimously adhered to the form of belief established at Nicaea.*" Sozom. vi. 23. ["Not long after, Liberius (the Pope) was recalled and re-instated in his see; for the people of Rome, *having raised a sedition, and expelled* Felix (whom the Arian party had intruded) from their Church, Constantius deemed it *inexpedient to provoke the popular fury.*" Socr. ii. 37.]

"Liberius, returning to Rome, found the *mind of the mass of men alienated from him,* because he had so shamefully yielded to Constantius. And thus it came to pass, that those persons who had hitherto kept aloof from Felix (the rival Pope), and had avoided his communion in favour of Liberius, on hearing what had happened, *left him for Felix,* who raised the Catholic standard. [Among others, Damasus (afterwards Pope) took the side of Felix. Such had been, even from the times of the Apostles, *the love of Catholic*

discipline in the Roman people."] Baron. ann. 357. ⟨56⟩ He
tells us besides ⟨57⟩, that the people would not even go to
the public baths, lest they should bathe with the party of
Liberius.

19. MILAN. "At the council of Milan, Eusebius of
Vercellae, when it was proposed to draw up a declaration
against Athanasius, said that the council ought first to be
sure of the faith of the Bishops attending it, for he had
found out that some of them were polluted with heresy.
Accordingly he brought before the Fathers the Nicene
creed, and said he was willing to comply with all their demands, after they had subscribed that confession. Dionysius, Bishop of Milan, at once took up the paper and began
to write his assent; but Valens (the Arian) violently pulled
pen and paper out of his hands, crying out that such a
course of proceeding was impossible. Whereupon, after
much tumult, *the question came before the people, and
great was the distress of all of them;* the faith of the Church
was [impugned][1] by the Bishops. *They then, dreading the
judgment of the people,* transfer their meeting from the
church to the imperial palace." Hilar. *ad Const.* i. ⟨8⟩.

"As the feast of Easter approached, the empress sent to
St. Ambrose to ask a church of him, where the Arians who
attended her might meet together. He replied, that a Bishop
could not give up the temple of God. The pretorian prefect
came into the church, where St. Ambrose was, *attended by
the people,* and endeavoured to persuade him to yield up
at least the Portian Basilica. *The people were clamorous
against the proposal;* and the prefect retired to report how
matters stood to the emperor. The Sunday following, St.

[1] impugned] attacked

Ambrose was explaining the creed, when he was informed that the officers were hanging up the imperial hangings in the Portian Basilica, and that upon this news the people were repairing thither. While he was offering up the holy sacrifice, a second message came that the *people had seized an Arian priest* as he was passing through the street. He despatched a number of his clergy to the spot to *rescue the Arian from his danger*. The court looked on this resistance of the people as seditious, and immediately laid considerable fines upon *the whole body of the tradesmen* of the city. Several were thrown into prison. In three days' time these tradesmen were fined two hundred pounds weight of gold, and they said *that they were ready to give as much again, on condition that they might retain their faith.* The prisons were filled with tradesmen : *all the officers of the household,* secretaries, agents of the emperor, and dependent officers who served under various counts, were kept within doors, and were forbidden to appear in public under pretence that they should bear no part in [the] sedition. *Men of higher rank* were menaced with severe consequences, unless the Basilica were surrendered. ...

"Next morning the Basilica was surrounded by soldiers; but it was reported, that *these soldiers had sent to the emperor to tell him* that if he wished to come abroad he might, and that they would attend him, if he was going to the assembly of the Catholics; otherwise, that they *would go to that which would be held by St. Ambrose.* Indeed, the *soldiers were all Catholics,* as well as the citizens of Milan; there were no heretics there, except a few officers of the emperor and some Goths. ...

"St. Ambrose was continuing his discourse when he was

told that the emperor had withdrawn the soldiers from the Basilica, and that he had restored to the tradesmen the fines which he had exacted from them. *This news gave joy to the people,* who expressed their delight with applauses and thanksgivings; *the soldiers themselves were eager to bring the news,* throwing themselves on the altars, and kissing them in token of peace." Fleury's *Hist.* xviii. 41, 42, Oxf. trans.

[20. THE SOLDIERY. Soldiers having been mentioned in the foregoing extract, I add the following passage. "Terentius, a general distinguished by his valour and by his piety, was able, on his return from Armenia, to erect trophies of victory. Valens promised to give him everything that he might desire. But he asked not for gold or silver, for lands, power, of honours; *he requested that a church might be given to those who preached the apostolical doctrines.*" Theodor. iv. 32.

"Valens sent Trajan, the general, against the barbarians. Trajan was defeated, and, on his return, the emperor reproached him severely, and accused him of weakness and cowardice. But Trajan replied with great boldness, 'It is not I, O emperor, who have been defeated; for you, *by fighting against God, have thrown the barbarians upon His protection.* Do you not know who those are whom you have driven from the churches, and who are those to whom you have given them up?' Arintheus and Victor, the other commanders, *accorded in what he had said,* and brought the emperor to reflect on the truth of their remonstrances." Ibid. 33.]

21. CHRISTENDOM GENERALLY. St. Hilary to Constantius: "Not only in words, but in tears, we beseech

you to save the Catholic Churches from any longer continu-
ance of these most grievous injuries, and of their present
intolerable persecutions and insults, which moreover they
are enduring, which is monstrous, from our brethren. Surely
your clemency should listen to the *voice of those who cry
out so loudly*, 'I am a Catholic, I have no wish to be a
heretic.' It should seem equitable to your sanctity, most
glorious Augustus, that they who fear the Lord God and
His judgment should not be polluted and contaminated
with execrable blasphemies, but *should have liberty to
follow those Bishops and prelates* who observe inviolate
the laws of charity, and who desire a perpetual and sincere
peace. It is impossible, it is unreasonable, to mix true and
false, to confuse light and darkness, and bring into a union,
of whatever kind, night and day. *Give permission to the
populations to hear the teaching of the pastors whom they
have wished,* whom they fixed on, whom they have chosen,
to attend their celebration of the divine mysteries, to offer
prayers through them for your safety and prosperity."
ad Const. i. ⟨i.2.⟩

Now I know quite well what will be said to so elaborate
a collection of instances as I have been making. The "lector
benevolus" will quote against me the words of Cicero,
"Utitur in re non dubiâ testibus non necessariis." This is sure
to befall a man when he directs the attention of a friend
to any truth which hitherto he has thought little of. At
first, he seems to be hazarding a paradox, and at length to
be committing a truism. The hearer is first of all startled,
and then disappointed; he ends by asking, "Is this all?" It
is a curious phenomenon in the philosophy of the human

mind, that we often do not know whether we hold a point
or not, thought we hold it; but when our attention is once
drawn to it, then forthwith we find it so much part of ourselves, that we cannot recollect when we began to hold it,
and we conclude (with truth), and we declare, that it has
always been our belief. Now it strikes me as worth noticing,
that, though Father Perrone is so clear upon the point of
doctrine which I have been urging in 1847, yet in 1842,
which is the date of my own copy of his *Praelectiones*, he
has not given the *consensus fidelium* any distinct place in
his *Loci Theologici*, though he has even given "heretici"
a place there. Among the *Media Traditionis*, he enumerates
the *magisterium* of the Church, the Acts of the Martyrs.
the Liturgy, usages and rites of worship, the Fathers, heretics, Church history; but not a word, that I can find, directly
and separately, about the *sensus fidelium*. This is the more
remarkable, because, speaking of the *Acta Martyrum*, he
gives a reason for the force of the testimony of the martyrs
which belongs quite as fully to the faithful generally; viz.
that, as not being theologians, they can only repeat that
objective truth, which, on the other hand, Fathers and
theologians do but present subjectively, and thereby
coloured with their own mental peculiarities. "We learn
from them," he says, "what was the traditionary doctrine in
both domestic and public assemblies of the Church, without any admixture of private and (so to say) subjective
explanation, such as at times creates a difficulty in ascertaining the real meaning of the Fathers; and so much the
more, because many of them were either women or
ordinary and untaught laymen, who brought out and
avowed just what they believed in a straightforward in-

artificial way." May we not conjecture that the argument from the Consent of the Faithful was but dimly written among the *Loci* on the tablets of his intellect, till the necessities, or rather the requirements, of the contemplated definition of the Immaculate Conception brought the argument before him with great force? Yet who will therefore for an instant suppose that he did not always hold it? Perhaps I have overlooked some passage of his treatises, and am in consequence interpreting his course of thought wrongly; but, at any rate, what I seem to see in him, is what actually does occur from time to time in myself and others. A man holds an opinion or a truth, yet without holding it with a simple consciousness and a direct recognition; and thus, though he had never denied, he has never gone so far as to profess it.

As to the particular doctrine to which I have here been directing my view, and the passage in history by which I have been illustrating it, I am not supposing that such times as the Arian will ever come again. As to the present, certainly, if there ever was an age which might dispense with the testimony of the faithful, and leave the maintenance of the truth to the pastors of the Church, it is the age in which we live. Never was the Episcopate of Christendom so devoted to the Holy See, so religious, so earnest in the discharge of its special duties, so little disposed to innovate, so superior to the temptation of theological sophistry. And perhaps this is the reason why the "consensus fidelium" has, in the minds of many, fallen into the background. Yet each constituent portion of the Church has its proper functions, and no portion can safely be neglected. Though the laity be but the reflection or echo of the clergy in matters of faith, yet there is something in the "pastorum et fidelium *conspiratio*," which is not in the pastors alone. The history of the definition of the Immaculate Conception shows us this; and it will be one among the blessings which the Holy Mother, who is the subject of it, will gain for us, in repayment of the definition, that by that very definition we are all reminded of the part which the laity have had in the preliminaries of its promulgation. Pope Pius has given us a pattern, in his manner of defining, of the duty of considering the sentiments of the laity upon a point of tradition, in spite of whatever fullness of evidence the Bishops had already thrown upon it.

In most cases when a definition is contemplated, the laity will have a testimony to give; but if ever there be an instance when they ought to be consulted, it is in the case of doctrines which bear directly upon devotional sentiments. Such is the Immaculate Conception, of which the *Rambler* was speaking in the sentence which has occasioned these remarks. The faithful people have ever a special function in regard to those doctrinal truths which relate to the Objects of worship. Hence it is, that, while the Councils of the fourth century were traitors to our Lord's divinity, the laity vehemently protested against its impugners. Hence it is, that, in a later age, when the learned Benedictines of Germany and France were perplexed in their enunciation of the doctrine of the Real Presence, Paschasius was supported by the faithful in his maintenance of it. The saints, again, are the object of a religious *cultus;* and therefore it was the faithful, again, who urged on the Holy See, in the time of John XXII., to declare their beatitude in heaven, though so many Fathers spoke variously. And the Blessed

Virgin is preëminently an object of devotion; and therefore it is, I repeat, that though Bishops had already spoken in favour of her absolute sinlessness, the Pope was not content without knowing the feelings of the faithful.

Father Dalgairns gives us another case in point; and with his words I conclude: "While devotion in the shape of a dogma issues from the high places of the Church, in the shape of devotion . . . it starts from below. . . . Place yourselves, in imagination, in a vast city of the East in the fifth century. Ephesus, the capital of Asia Minor, is all in commotion; for a council is to be held there, and Bishops are flocking in from all parts of the world. There is anxiety painted on every face; so that you may easily see that the question is one of general interest. . . . Ask the very children in the streets what is the matter; they will tell you that wicked men are coming to make out that their own mother is not the Mother of God. And so, during a livelong day of June, they crowd around the gates of the old cathedral-church of St. Mary, and watch with anxious faces each Bishop as he goes in. Well might they be anxious; for it is well known that Nestorius has won the court over to his side. It was only the other day that he entered the town, with banners displayed and trumpets sounding, surrounded by the glittering files of the emperor's body-guard, with Count Candidianus, their general and his own partisan, at their head. Besides which, it is known for certain, that at least eighty-four Bishops are ready to vote with him; and who knows how many more? He is himself the patriarch of Constantinople, the rival of Rome, the imperial city of the East; and then John of Antioch is hourly expected with his quota of votes; and he, the patriarch of the see next in

influence to that of Nestorius, is, if not a heretic, at least of
that wretched party which, in ecclesiastical disputes, ever
hovers between the two camps of the devil and of God.
The day wears on, and still nothing issues from the church;
it proves, at least, that there is a difference of opinion; and
as the shades of evening close around them, the weary
watchers grow more anxious still. At length the great gates
of the Basilica are thrown open; and oh, what a cry of joy
bursts from the assembled crowd, as it is announced to them
that Mary has been proclaimed to be, what every one with a
Catholic heart knew that she was before, the Mother of
God! . . . Men, women, and children, the noble and the
low-born, the stately matron and the modest maiden, all
crowd round the Bishops with acclamations. They will not
leave them; they accompany them to their homes with a
long procession of lighted torches; they burn incense before
them, after the eastern fashion, to do them honour. There
was but little sleep in Ephesus that night; for very joy they
remained awake; the whole town was one blaze of light,
for each window was illuminated."[1]

My own drift is somewhat different from that which has
dictated this glowing description; but the substance of the
argument of each of us is one and the same. I think certainly that the *Ecclesia docens* is more happy when she
has such enthusiastic partisans about her as are here represented, than when she cuts off the faithful from the study
of her divine doctrines and the sympathy of her divine
contemplations, and requires from them a *fides implicita* in
her word, which in the educated classes will terminate in
indifference, and in the poorer in superstition.   O.

[1] Sacred Heart

THE ORTHODOXY
OF THE BODY OF THE FAITHFUL
DURING THE SUPREMACY OF ARIANISM

Appendix V
to the third edition (1871) of
THE ARIANS OF THE FOURTH CENTURY

THE ORTHODOXY OF THE BODY OF THE FAITHFUL DURING THE SUPREMACY OF ARIANISM

THIS NOTE was added as an appendix to the third edition of *The Arians of the Fourth Century* in 1871, pp. 445-68. It consists of parts of the *Rambler* article in a condensed form; but its importance chiefly rests in its conclusion, in which Newman answers his critics.

The text is as follows : —

The episcopate, whose action was so prompt and concordant at Nicaea on the rise of Arianism, did not, as a class or order of men, play a good part in the troubles consequent upon the Council; and the laity did. The Catholic people, in the length and breadth of Christendom, were the obstinate champions of Catholic truth, and the bishops were not. Of course there were great and illustrious exceptions; first, Athanasius, Hilary, the Latin Eusebius, and Phoebadius; and after them, Basil, the two Gregories, and Ambrose; there are others, too, who suffered, if they did nothing else, as Eustathius, Paulus, Paulinus, and Dionysius; and the Egyptian bishops, whose weight was small in the Church in proportion to the great power of their Patriarch. And, on the other hand, as I shall say presently, there were excep-

tions to the Christian heroism of the laity, especially in
some of the great towns. And again, in speaking of the
laity, I speak inclusively of their parish-priests (so to call
them), at least in many places; but on the whole, taking
a wide view of the history, we are obliged to say that the
governing body of the Church came short, and the
governed were pre-eminent in faith, zeal, courage, and
constancy.

This is a very remarkable fact : but there is a moral in
it. Perhaps it was permitted, in order to impress upon the
Church at that very time passing out of her state of persecution to her long temporal ascendancy, the great
evangelical lesson, that, not the wise and powerful, but
the obscure, the unlearned, and the weak constitute her
real strength. It was mainly by the faithful people that
Paganism was overthrown; it was by the faithful people,
under the lead of Athanasius and the Egyptian bishops,
and in some places supported by their Bishops or priests,
that the worst of heresies was withstood and stamped out
of the sacred territory.

The contrast stands as follows : ——

Newman now proceeds to cite the evidences for his claim
that the body of the Bishops failed in their confession of the
faith and that there was a temporary suspense of the functions of the Ecclesia docens. The text of 1871 (its correc-
tions, suppressions and additions) can be reconstructed by
referring to pages 77-86 supra, omitting all material in
square brackets, and including all material in triangular
brackets, and all footnotes.

Newman provides the second section of proofs—those of the fidelity of the laity—with a new introduction. Its text is as follows : —

Coming to the opposite side of the contrast, I observe that there were great efforts made on the part of the Arians to render their heresy popular. Arius himself, according to the Arian Philostorgius, "wrote songs for the sea, and for the mill, and for the road, and then set them to suitable music."[1] Hist. ii. 2. Alexander speaks of the "running about" of the Arian women, Theod. Hist. i. 4, and of the buffoonery of their men. Socrates says that "in the Imperial court, the officers of the bedchamber held disputes with the women, and in the city, in every house, there was a war of dialectics," ii. 2. Especially at Constantinople there were as Gregory says, "of Jezebels as thick a crop as of hemlock in a field," Orat. 35, 3; and he himself suffered from the popular violence there. At Alexandria the Arian women are described by Athanasius as "running up and down like Bacchanals and furies," and as "passing that day in grief on which they could do no harm." *Hist. Arian.* 59.

The controversy was introduced in ridicule into the heathen theatres, Euseb. v. Const. ii. 6. Socr. i. 6. "Men of yesterday," says Gregory Nyssen, "mere mechanics, off-hand dogmatists in theology, servants too and slaves that have been scourged, run-aways from servile work, and philosophical about things incomprehensible. Of such the city is full; its entrances, forums, squares,

---

[1] The translations which follow are for the most part from Bohn's and the Oxford editions, the passages being abridged.

thoroughfares; the clothes-vendors, the money-lenders, the victuallers. Ask about pence, and they will discuss the generate and ingenerate," etc., etc., tom. ii. p.898. Socrates, too, says that the heresy "ravaged provinces and cities"; and Theodoret that, "quarrels took place in every city and village concerning the divine dogma, the people looking on, and taking sides." *Hist.* i. 6.

In spite of these attempts, however, on the part of the Arians, still, viewing Christendom as a whole, we shall find that the Catholic populations sided with Athanasius; and the fierce disputes above described evidenced the zeal of the orthodox rather than the strength of the heretical party.

This will appear in the following extracts : ——

The 1871 version of the proofs which follow can, as before, be re-constructed by referring to pages 86-101 supra, omitting all material in square brackets, and including all material in triangular brackets, and all footnotes.

The remainder of the *Rambler* article was not re-printed, but the 1871 version concludes with the following answer by Newman to his critics : —

In drawing out this comparison between the conduct of the Catholic Bishops and that of their flocks during the Arian troubles, I must not be understood as intending any conclusion inconsistent with the infallibility of the Ecclesia docens, (that is, the Church when teaching) and with the claim of the Pope and the Bishops to constitute the Church in that aspect. I am led to give this caution, because, for the want of it, I was seriously misunderstood in some quarters on my first writing on the above subject in the *Rambler* Magazine of May, 1859. But on that occasion I was writing simply historically, not doctrinally, and, while it is historically true, it is in no sense doctrinally false, that a Pope, as a private doctor, and much more Bishops, when not teaching formally, may err, as we find they did err in the fourth century. Pope Liberius might sign a Eusebian formula at Sirmium, and the mass of Bishops at Ariminum or elsewhere, and yet they might, in spite of this error, be infallible in their *ex cathedra* decisions.

The reason of my being misunderstood arose from two or three clauses or expressions which occurred in the course of my remarks, which I should not have used had I anticipated how they would be taken, and which I avail myself of this opportunity to explain and withdraw. First, I will quote the passage which bore a meaning which I certainly did not intend, and then I will note the phrases which seem to have given this meaning to it. It will be seen how little, when those phrases are withdrawn, the sense of the passage, as I intended it, is affected by the withdrawal. I said then : —

"It is not a little remarkable, that, though, historically speaking, the fourth century is the age of doctors, illustrated, as it is, by the Saints Athanasius, Hilary, the two Gregories, Basil, Chrysostom, Ambrose, Jerome, and Augustine, (and all those saints bishops also), except one, nevertheless in that very day the Divine tradition committed to the infallible Church was proclaimed and maintained far more by the faithful than by the Episcopate.

"Here of course I must explain :—in saying this then, undoubtedly I am not denying that the great body of the Bishops were in their internal belief orthodox; nor that there were numbers of clergy who stood by the laity and acted as their centres and guides; nor that the laity actually received their faith, in the first instance, from the Bishops and clergy; nor that some portions of the laity were ignorant, and other portions were at length corrupted by the Arian teachers, who got possession of the sees, and ordained an heretical clergy :—but I mean still, that in that time of immense confusion the divine dogma of our Lord's divinity was proclaimed, enforced, maintained, and (humanly speaking) preserved, far more by the 'Ecclesia docta' than by the 'Ecclesia docens'; that the body of the Episcopate was unfaithful to its commission, while the body of the laity was faithful to its baptism; that at one time the pope, at other times a patriarchal, metropolitan, or other great see, at other times general councils, said what they should not have said, or did what obscured and compromised revealed truth; while, on the other hand, it was the Christian people, who, under Providence, were the ecclesiastical strength of Athanasius, Hilary, Eusebius of Vercellae, and other great solitary confessors, who would have failed without them. . . .

"On the one hand, then, I say, that there was a temporary suspense of the functions of the 'Ecclesia docens'. The body of Bishops failed in their confession of the faith. They spoke variously, one against another; there was nothing, after Nicaea, of firm, unvarying, consistent testimony, for nearly sixty years. . . .

"We come secondly to the proofs of the fidelity of the laity, and the effectiveness of that fidelity, during that domination of Imperial heresy, to which the foregoing passages have related."

The three clauses which furnished matter of objection were these : —I said, (1) that "there was a temporary suspense of the functions of the 'Ecclesia docens' "; (2) that "the body of Bishops failed in their confession of the faith". (3) that "general councils, etc., said what they should not have said, or did what obscured and compromised revealed truth".

(1) That "there was a temporary *suspense* of the functions of the Ecclesia docens" is not true, if by saying so is meant that the Council of Nicaea held in 325 did not sufficiently define and promulgate for all times and all places the dogma of our Lord's divinity, and that the notoriety of that Council and the voices of its great supporters and maintainers, as Athanasius, Hilary, etc., did not bring home the dogma to the intelligence of the faithful in all parts of Christendom. But what I meant by "suspense" (I did not say "suspension", purposely) was only this, that there was no authoritative utterance of the Church's infallible voice in matter of fact between the Nicene Council, AD. 325, and the Council of Constantinople, A.D. 381, or, in the words which I actually used, "there was nothing after Nicaea of firm, unvarying, consistent testimony for nearly sixty years". As writing before the Vatican Definition of 1870, I did not lay stress

upon the Roman Councils under Popes Julius and Damasus.[1]

(2) That "the *body* of Bishops failed in their confession of the faith", p. 17. Here, if the word "body" is used in the sense of the Latin "corpus", as "corpus" is used in theological treatises, and as it doubtless would be translated for the benefit of readers ignorant of the English language, certainly this would be a heretical statement. But I meant nothing of the kind. I used it in the vague, familiar, genuine sense of which Johnson gives instances in his dictionary as meaning "the great preponderance", or, "the mass" of Bishops, viewing them in the main or the gross, as a *cumulus* of individuals. Thus Hooker says, "Life and death have divided between them the whole body of mankind"; Clarendon, after speaking of the van of the king's army says, "in the body was the

[1] A distinguished theologian infers from my words that I deny that "the Church is in every time the activum instrumentum docendi." But I do not admit the fairness of this inference. Distinguo: activum instrumentum docendi virtuale, C. Actuale, N. The Ecumenical Council of 325 was an effective authority in 341, 351, and 359, though at those dates the Arians were in the seats of teaching. Fr. Perrone agrees with me. (1). He reckons the "fidelium sensus" among the "instrumenta traditionis." (*Immac. Concept.* p. 139). (2). He contemplates, nay he instances, the case in which the " sensus fidelium" supplies, as the "instrumentum," the absence of the other instruments, the *magisterium* of the Church, as exercised at Nicaea, being always supposed. One of his instances is that of the dogma de visione Dei beatifica. He says: "Certe quidem in Ecclesia non deerat quoad hunc fidei articulum divina traditio; alioquin, nunquam is definiri potuisset: verum non omnibus illa erat comperta: divina eloquia haud satis in re sunt conspicua; Patres, ut vidimus, in varias abierunt sententias; liturgiae ipsae non modicam prae se ferunt difficultatem. His omnibus succurrit juge Ecclesiae magisterium; communis praeterea fidelium sensus." p.148.

king and the prince" : and Addison speaks of "navigable rivers, which ran up into the body of Italy". In this sense it is true historically that the body of Bishops failed in their confession. Tillemont, quoting from St. Gregory Nazianzen, says, "La souscription (Arienne) était une des dispositions necessaires pour entrer et pour se conserver dans l'episcopat. L'encre était toujours toute prête, et l'accusateur aussi. Ceux qui avaient paru invincibles jusques alors, céderent à cette tempête. Si leur esprit ne tomba pas dans l'heresie, leur main néanmoins y consentit. ... Peu d'Evêques s'exemterent de ce malheur, n'y ayant eu que ceux que leur propre bassesse faisait negliger, ou que leur vertu fit resister genereusement, et que Dieu conserva afin qu'il restât encore quelque semence et quelque racine pour faire refleurir Israel." T. vi. p.499. In St. Gregory's own words πλῆν ὀλίγων ἄγαν, πάντες τοῦ καιροῦ γεγόνασι τοσοῦτον ἀλλήλων διενεγκόντες, ὅσον τοὺς μὲν πρότερον, τοὺς δὲ ὕστερον τοῦτο παθεῖν. Orat. xxi. 24. p. 401. Ed. Bened.

(3) That "*general* councils said what they should not have said, and did what obscured and compromised revealed truth." Here again the question to be determined is what is meant by the word "general". If I meant by "general" ecumenical, I should have spoken as no Catholic can speak; but ecumenical Councils there were none between 325 and 381, and so I could not be referring to any; and in matter of fact I used the word "general" in *contrast* to "ecumenical", as I had used it in Tract No. 90, and as Bellarmine uses the word. He makes a fourfold division of "general Councils", viz., those which are approbata; reprobata; partim confirmata, partim repro-

bata; and nec manifeste probata nec manifeste reprobata. Among the "reprobata" he placed the Arian Councils. They were quite large enough to be called "generalia"; the twin Councils of Seleucia and Ariminum numbering as many as 540 Bishops. When I spoke then of "general councils compromising revealed truth", I spoke of the Arian or Eusebian Councils, not of the Catholic.

I hope this is enough to observe on this subject.